ORDINARY BOYS
THE CLASS OF '79

ORDINARY BOYS

THE CLASS OF '79

Merv Payne

First published in Great Britain in 2020
Copyright © Merv Payne 2020

Merv Payne has asserted his right under the Copyright, Designs and Patents Act 1988 to be identified as the author of this work.

All rights reserved. No part of this publication may be reproduced, distributed, or transmitted in any form or by any means, including photocopying, recording, or other electronic or mechanical methods, without the prior written permission of the author.

Every reasonable effort has been made to trace copyright holders of material reproduced in this book, but if any have been inadvertently overlooked, the author would be glad to hear from them.

ISBN: 9781653302536

Acknowledgements

The task of revisiting a football season over 40 years ago would have been hard enough if this book had been about the first team of a professional football club, but researching the youth team record would have been completely impossible without the amazing assistance of so many people.

Thanks to the power of Facebook which introduced me to Chris Bethell and Phil Coleman, I was able to track down and speak to almost every member of the squad and every single one I spoke to - whilst the memory for some was understandably sketchy - were fantastically co-operative.

I have to first thank both Chris and Phil for the contacts but also Phil for his in-depth knowledge of the era in general and a whole host of photographic memorabilia. Chris has also been very helpful in providing photographs so vital to rekindling that special time.

In no particular order, I'd like to thank Peter Gleasure, Dave Martin, Paul Roberts, Paul Robinson, Tony Kinsella, Dave Mehmet, Chris Dibble, David Payne, Alan McKenna, Kevin O'Callaghan and Vince Hilaire. All of them were extremely generous in giving up their time to talk to me after being relentlessly pestered by me by text or WhatsApp.

For those I was unable to get in touch with, my apologies, do get in touch, I'd be happy to add your story!

Contents

	Introduction	1
Chapter 1	Punk Football	7
Chapter 2	Humble Beginnings	13
Chapter 3	Enter Oscar	23
Chapter 4	Fifteen Minutes of Infamy	33
Chapter 5	Out of the Frying Pan	49
Chapter 6	All Change	61
Chapter 7	"Mr Clough to You…"	75
Chapter 8	Boys to Men	87
Chapter 9	The Class of '79	95
Chapter 10	Look at What You Could Have Won	109
Chapter 11	From Cleaning Kitch's Boots to the UEFA Cup	117
Chapter 12	Throwing It All Away	125
Chapter 13	And Then There Was One	137
Chapter 14	The Bitter End	163
Chapter 15	When Life Gives You Lemons…	175

Extra Time
Full Circle 189
Dean Horrix 193
George Petchey 197
A Different Game 203
The FA Youth Cup 210

Introduction

This book is about football in a time so far removed from today's game that it almost seems like a different sport altogether.

It is about a time when if, as a football-mad kid you felt you were good enough to make the grade and be a professional footballer, you could write a letter to your local club and get a trial. Of course that rarely worked!

It was a time when you could enjoy your football at whichever level you wanted to play it. Whether it was in the local park or estate with your friends for an impromptu kick-about, at school in the playground or for the school team or with a local club on a Saturday or Sunday morning. It truly was a game for ordinary boys.

The dream to play football for a living was every bit as strong back in the 1970s as it is today, but the path to realising that dream a world away, as was the incentive. In the 1970s and before, football clubs didn't have a fraction of the power and influence that they do today. They weren't able to 'sign' schoolboy footballers until they had virtually left school.

Today, they are scouted at the age of five or six - and often back on the scrap heap before they reach their teens.

Young footballers were able to prove their ability by progressing through the schools, district and county system and whilst it seems very old-fashioned these days, it was a very good way of sifting talent from various geographical regions of the country to the top.

Scouts would simply turn up at district schools cup finals, or county matches.

Many will say that the current system is better because it teaches young footballers the right habits at an early age and prevents bad habits forming that will hamper their progress. Footballers themselves might disagree.

Maybe the best habit any child can learn in a sport is to love the game. If you've been coached and coached for as long as you can remember, forbidden from playing with your mates in your school or local junior team and have an army of track-suited, clipboard-wielding robots obsessing over your height every six months, it's easy to see why so many young footballers fall out of love with the game very quickly.

This is the story of a particular crop of ordinary boys. Football-mad lads who always had a ball at their feet. They loved the game - and the game loved them right back. From the rough, dusty streets and grey concrete estates of south and east London to the comparative luxury of training with professional football clubs on local parks - and even stadium forecourts, they were able to play the game the way they wanted to play it.

These days, professional clubs have teams progressing at almost every age group right up to their Academy, development or Under 23 squads. Everything is carefully monitored, which obviously has to be a good thing.

The structure of professional football in the 70s could see a player still at school playing a Midweek League (reserve) match up against a 35-year-old veteran of several hundred games fighting for his place back in the first team. Sometimes fighting was exactly what he did too.

Was it the same for every team? There was still a hierarchy of course. The Manchester Uniteds, Liverpools and Arsenals were nowhere near the financial powerhouses they are today, but they still had money. They still had attendances of 40,000 at every home match which kept the coffers nicely filled and allowed them to invest in youth policies and the sort of facilities that clubs like Millwall cold only dream about.

But fortunately, back in the 1970s, it wasn't all about money, I mean, let's face it, pretty much everyone was skint in the 70s weren't they? They just didn't really give a toss about it.

As is often the case, it was the ones that didn't have the riches that improvised, grafted harder, and used their brains while the more fortunate ones became complacent. More often than not, it worked. Everyone loves an underdog after all.

As a young footballer aged around 13 or 14, you could train with any number of clubs. You could be at Chelsea one night, Charlton the next, then Palace, then Millwall. It was very much a free-for-all.

The first commitment any club could get from a young player they wanted was to sign them on schoolboy forms and then they could offer them their first professional contract.

Once signed, there was no shortage of action for a young schoolboy or first year professional footballer. League action came in the form of the regional South East Counties League which had its own League Cup and also the Southern Junior Floodlit Cup competition. But the big one, as is (just about) still the case today in the senior game, was the FA Cup - or FA Youth Cup.

Like its senior counterpart, it is a nationwide competition and sees around 400 clubs enter players aged between 15 and 18 every year.

Started in 1951, it was understandably dominated by the giants of the game at the time with Manchester United winning the first five finals. It took ten years for a team outside the top flight to win it when Second Division Newcastle lifted the trophy in 1962, it was another ten years before Third Division champions Aston Villa won it as the first team from outside the top two, but it continued to be dominated by the major names in the game.

The mid seventies would prove to be a breeding ground for talent bursting through from the lower leagues to grace the top flight in the eighties and Second Division West Brom won the final to go alongside their promotion place in 1976, a team that would go on to produce several stars of one of the club's most successful teams of recent times.

Crystal Palace then won back-to-back finals as a Third Division and then Second Division club in 1977 and 1978 with a team that would go on to grace the top flight and be dubbed 'The Team of the Eighties', this only served to cement the reputation of the competition as being a precursor to the talented players - and teams of the future.

When Millwall entered the competition for the 1978-79 season as a Second Division team, only four different teams from outside the top division had managed to win the competition. On each of those four occasions, their respective first teams had been promoted to the First Division soon after.

In an era long before £100 million intercontinental transfer deals, talented youth football was by no means a certain route to the top, but it was a bloody good bet.

Back in the mid 1970s all aspiring young footballers were ordinary boys. There was nothing different in that respect about the group of young players turning up for training at Millwall. Once they were together as a team though, it was a very different matter.

There's probably no need for a spoiler alert at this point, as it's probably quite obvious that, as is so often the case at Millwall, things didn't quite go to plan - but there is so much more to tell than that.

This is the story about a remarkable group of young footballers and their journey.

1

Punk Football

By the summer of 1978 Millwall Football Club had begun one of its many periods of decline. It was a scenario familiar to all of its long-suffering fans.

Like punk bursting onto the music scene, it was seemingly on the verge of an exciting new era one minute, condemned and spiralling downward the next.

The 1960s had brought an upsurge in fortunes at The Den which matched the positivity and progress of the swinging era. They started the decade in football's newly-formed Division Four basement following a depressing spell of post-war third tier football famine.

The Second World War had brought the game to a halt just as The Lions were looking to take their place at the top of the game.

They reached an FA Cup semi-final in 1938 as a third tier team on their way to the Division Three South title under the management of the mercurial Charlie

Hewitt and consolidated an impressive mid-table place in Division Two the following year.

Looking set for a tilt at the top division less than 20 years after joining the league, regular football was suspended at the outbreak of War and by the time they reconvened at a bomb-damaged Den in 1946-47 the team was a shadow of its pre-war power and relegated in only the second regular peacetime season.

It would be another 20 years before the club was in a position to even consider hosting First Division football.

As the 60s ended, Millwall supporters could only watch on in envy as local rivals Crystal Palace stole their thunder and prevented them from completing the journey from Fourth to First Divisions in a handful of seasons.

Benny Fenton's young Lions had all the swagger and panache of the late 60s and early 70s London scene, but not quite as much as their rivals up west. Chelsea plucked Millwall hero Keith Weller to add to their FA Cup-chasing squad. It was a loss that, in most Lions fans' eyes, deprived them once more of that elusive top flight place.

There was another near miss in 1972 when a third place finish wasn't enough with only two teams being promoted and relegated from the Second Division and there must have been some hollow ironic laughs that were so familiar amidst the gallows humour that permeated The Den terraces when, in 1975, Millwall were relegated after finishing third from bottom.

The league had decided to change the amount of teams promoted and relegated at the start of the 73-74 season which meant that in 1975 The Lions found themselves in Division Three. Had that rule change came about two years earlier it would have been the First not Third where Millwall fans watched their team.

It was a twist of fate that was becoming all too familiar for the long-suffering denizens of SE16.

Thankfully, under a bright, forward-thinking new young manager in Gordon Jago, Millwall were able to bounce straight back with promotion in 1976 and with the country temporarily out of the doldrums once more too, the momentum gained from that surprise rise looked to be taking them once more to the edge of glory.

They couldn't quite make it in 1976-77 but giving eventual champions and runners-up Wolves and Chelsea the games of their lives gave genuine hope that a tenth place finish could be bettered with promotion in 1978.

Everything at the club was in place. 1977-78 was going to be Millwall's time to make the headlines. That is exactly what happened, but for all the wrong reasons. Millwall had always had an element of trouble attached to it, little more than anyone else at the time, but one television programme broadcast in mid-November 1977 was to change all of that for good.

The BBC were allowed access to Millwall Football Club with Jago's blessing, under what would turn out to be the completely false premise of showing what the club were doing to forge a bond with its supporters and local community.

Ignoring the club's pleas not to broadcast when they strongly objected to its final viewing of the coverage, the end result was an edition of Panorama, first aired on 14th November 1977, which only served to demonise the club as a leader in the worrying rapid rise of organised violence at football. It put faces and names to this latest scourge of British society.

The establishment were already turning their noses up at Punk, seeing it as an unwanted distraction during a Silver Jubilee year as the country tried to pull itself out of the early seventies downturn.

Millwall was, almost overnight, synonymous with everything that was bad about football. It was a brutal wound that it still bears the scars of today and one that is all too frequently opened and salted. 77-78 was going wrong on the pitch too.

The expected continued momentum from the previous season didn't materialise and just to compound the club's misery, even their best run in the FA Cup ended in televised disaster.

As if to prove the lopsided Panorama narrative, Millwall's 6-1 quarter final drubbing at home to Ipswich was played out to a backdrop of continual disorder – all in front of the cameras.

It had long since proved too much for Jago who left for the USA, disillusioned with the game in the UK soon after the Panorama programme aired. Jago's legacy in this country was not only helping the development of an exciting QPR team that almost won the First Division title in 1976, but an all-round talent for developing young players that was years ahead of his time.

Under the stewardship of George Petchey, The Lions managed to avoid the drop but with heavy FA sanctions hanging over them as a result of the Ipswich trouble, the club began the 1978-79 season well and truly slumped in its lowest decline for thirty years.

Thankfully though, it wasn't all doom and gloom.

Ordinary Boys

Humble Beginnings

The path to fulfilling your dreams of becoming a professional footballer in the 1970s was about as far removed from the journey today as it's possible to be, as was the motivation. Ask any six-year-old right now who has been scouted by Manchester City, Arsenal or Chelsea if they want to play football for a living because they love the game and of course they'll tell you that is the case.

They'll no doubt also enjoy informing you what their favourite colour is, their bestest friend in the whole wide world at school, and their favourite character on Paw Patrol.

If, at the ripe old age of eight, nine or ten, they're still lucky enough to be on the books at The Etihad, The Emirates or Stamford Bridge, they may already be well on their way to becoming a cynical junior 'pro', with enough matches under their belt to have a slightly jaded view of 'the game'.

By now of course, the realisation will have dawned on them that football is a serious business, a short career where you have to earn as much money as possible and take every chance that comes your way.

You might think that's a slightly brutal and over-exaggerated view of the game today. I'm sure any parents who have boys and girls playing the game at any level will defend the various well-organised, carefully sanctioned and closely scrutinised junior football clubs and protest that the fast car, get super-rich quick, WAG culture of the game is quickly being consigned to a naïve and slightly embarrassing period of early millennial history, but it's left an indelible scar.

The ever increasing coverage, wealth and celebrity in the game today will ensure that, even though the Citys, Uniteds, Arsenals, Chelseas and Liverpools of the world have recognised the need to manage expectation and aspiration, the dream of playing football for a living today is akin to a young boy back in the early seventies harbouring hopes of walking on the moon.

In 1971, boys still yearned to be train drivers as much as professional footballers, and those who hoped to play the game as a job did so very much out of pure passion for the game and nothing else.

Phil Coleman grew up with his two brothers Steve and Nicky in a humble council house on the Horn Park Estate in Lee, on the borders of the London boroughs of Lewisham and Bromley. His earliest memories are of playing football in the garden and local parks with his siblings and being held aloft on his dad's shoulders on the various terraces of London's football stadiums.

Despite their proximity to Millwall, Phil doesn't remember being taken to The Den by his dad who was more a lover of the game in general rather than a one-club man at the time. It would be Fulham one week, Charlton the next, then maybe Palace. Millwall would come into the young Phil's life soon enough though. His home life was secure, stable and supportive of whatever he wanted to do, and Phil just wanted to play sport – and mostly football. His first taste of organised matches was at the age of nine when he would play every Saturday for his primary school – Horn Park.

By his own modest admission, Phil "somehow managed" to pass his eleven plus which gave him the opportunity to join one of the local grammar schools. It was an easy choice to make.

John Roan school was a footballing school. In Phil's own words, it was football, football, football at The Roan. They put out six teams every weekend and their purpose-built facilities on Kidbrooke Park Road was the envy of every other school in the area in 1971.

For Phil, it was a ten-minute stroll from his family home every Saturday morning to make the 10am kick off. Initially, struggling to make the starting eleven meant he had to make do with a place between the sticks but he soon earned a place in the back four at left back.

A few months into this new sporting life which Phil was enjoying immensely, he was approached by a man who had some advice that would change Coleman's footballing path.

"I was approached by some old guy and he said: you should play centre back" Phil recalls.

That 'old guy' was Joe Broadfoot.

Joe Broadfoot was an ex Roan boy and had played as a winger for Millwall between 1958 and 1963. His 220 appearances and 60 goals caught the eye of Ipswich Town's new manager Jackie Milburn and the East Anglian side paid what was then a useful sum of £16,000 for his services. Ipswich were fighting to stay in the top flight after winning the title at their first attempt under Alf Ramsey two seasons before.

Now Ramsey had left to mastermind England's 1966 World Cup triumph and Ipswich were hurtling back to whence they came. There was a certain amount of irony that less than a decade after Broadfoot's advice, Coleman would be part of a team that would once again have Ipswich knocking on the Millwall door to plunder their young talent.

Broadfoot's word certainly held sway – even though the six teams were run by their own individual coach, overseen by the PE teacher and head teacher – and by the end of his first year Coleman was a regular at centre back for a Roan side that could name future pros such as Gary Micklewhite and Dave Campbell amongst their numbers and eventually formed what would prove to be a formidable and all-conquering under 19s team.

The game wasn't swarmed by commission-hungry scouts or vulture-like agents in the 70s. If you wanted to have any chance of being noticed by a professional club, you had to progress to the district and county teams.

Coleman represented Blackheath district and then London at County level – as well as playing at a high level of Sunday League - and then found himself as part of a team made up of talented under 16s, 17s and 18s entered for the national schools under 19s competition.

Roan made it to the last four where they faced the daunting prospect of Somerset Public school Millfield, yet they brushed them aside 6-1. For Coleman, that side had an inescapable air of invincibility about it for him and it was a feeling he was to experience again quite soon at a much higher level. The final was shrouded in controversy. Due to be played at Birmingham City's St Andrews stadium, Roan's opponents were St Phillip's College Edgbaston – virtually a goal kick away from the final venue.

An appeal by Roan's head for the venue to be moved was refused so he made sure 650 pupils were able to make the journey to cheer them on to a famous 4-1 victory. That wasn't the only stumbling block. Roan had to gain permission from Charlton to play Dave Campbell who by then was a first team regular at The Valley.

These days, the minute players are taken under the wing of a professional football academy they are restricted from playing football at the fun, enjoyable level of school or local junior league. Not only are they deprived of that enjoyable aspect of the game, but also the opportunity to experience the sort of progression, achievement and glory with their peers that the modern-day academy simply doesn't allow. In the 1970s football clubs had no power over the school system whatsoever, but that didn't mean they didn't get involved – and make some incredible demands on their young hopefuls.

At the age of 14, Coleman was training with Charlton, Millwall and Arsenal. The current closed shop whereby a child is contracted and has an agent tying him to a single club before he even knows what he wants for next Christmas let alone considering which career path to choose was a world away back then. Gary Micklewhite was being picked up by his dad after school on Friday afternoon, driving to Euston and catching the train to Manchester so that he could spend the weekend training with United before making the return trip Sunday evening in time for his Monday morning studies.

The only form of commitment then was to be offered schoolboy forms and for Coleman it was a no brainer. By the time he had to make the decision, he had been a regular on the Cold Blow Lane terrace at The Den for a few years and when Millwall's Ted Buxton and Billy Neil offered him the chance to sign for The Lions it was the easiest choice to make:

"I remember the first time I walked into The Den. I walked up those steps at the back of the Cold Blow Lane end at an evening game and saw this illuminated green baize of a pitch."

"Then I saw Barry Kitchener emerge from the tunnel, leading the team out, his long hair flowing, this absolute giant of a bloke and I thought: 'wow, that's for me'. That night I watched Kitch and Alan Dorney deal with everything and I just thought, 'that'll do', and before long I was cleaning Dorney's boots as a Millwall player on schoolboy forms". Phil Coleman joined Millwall aged 15 years and 3 months – which was the FA rule for the youngest age a player could be signed by a professional club.

Life as a Millwall schoolboy was training, training, training. Every day at the Peek Freans factory fields and at Crofton Park under Billy Neil.

By now, playing for Millwall in the South East Counties League on Saturday mornings largely replaced appearances for The Roan, probably the first instance of a professional club depriving a school of a player, although it no doubt would have been done with the blessing of the school, safe in the knowledge that there was a rich seam of footballing talent left to mine in south east London.

By 16, Coleman was starting to be selected for Millwall's Midweek League games which were, in his own words, brutal:

"You found yourself playing against the likes of Teddy Maybank of Brighton, top strikers, and they wouldn't mess around. The pitches were like bogs and you were facing two or three first team players looking to get back into their starting elevens." Phil recalls.

Billy Neil was a true Millwall legend. A terrace favourite whose career had been cruelly cut short by injury, he coached the schoolboys and youths at Millwall and Coleman clearly remembers how he had an aura about him that made you want to play for him. More than that, he looked out for the players, there was truly a family spirit at Millwall. It was a tough family but like all good clans, they looked out for one another. Neil would ferry the players from wherever they lived to the club's new training venue at Langley Park, nothing was too much trouble.

It nurtured what would be the nucleus of Millwall's all-conquering youth team of 1979. Several players, including Coleman, were offered apprenticeships following a successful five day tour of Belgium, and that's when the fun really began.

Ordinary Boys

3

Enter Oscar

Sport – especially football – has long provided the antidote to hard times. To quote Dickens, the 70s could certainly be described as the best of times and the worst of times.

The bust to the sixties boom, it was a decade where the UK's complacency would catch up with it. In a quite alarming mirror of recent times, there was a controversial referendum on the UK's relationship with Europe and racial tension had continued to build since Enoch Powell's infamous 'Rivers of Blood' speech at the end of the previous decade, widely believed to be the populist trigger to the Conservatives' 1970 general election victory.

Ted Heath's administration oversaw a three day week to combat the energy crisis, a financial crash and another Miners' strike. The conflict in Northern Ireland reached its bloodiest peak and the country seemed to be smashing its head on the self-destruct button. Labour didn't fair much better with Harold Wilson's 30% inflation and embarrassing IMF bailout. The country seemed to be lurching from one inept leader to another with no meaningful direction or useful majority to rule, like I said, it's an uncomfortably familiar story isn't it?

Thankfully there was a heat wave, punk and a stylish brand of football down at The Den to keep Millwall fans happy as the decade limped on. Britain's Winter of Discontent would turn in to a summer of joy in a small corner of south east London, but not before the hard work was put in.

No matter how much you love playing football, doing it for a living can become tiresome. Any professional footballer will tell you how much they hated pre-season training and Eamon Dunphy's superb, ground-breaking book 'Only A Game?' published in 1976, captured the vagaries of the slog perfectly.

At the time the book was published, Millwall had pulled themselves up by their bootstraps and, in the midst of a nosedive back through the league, had soared back into the Second Division under the guidance of Gordon Jago.

Their upward curve seemed to be relentless and could only possibly end at one glorious destination: The First Division. Not only were the first team getting admiring glances and nudging their way into the top half of the second tier by the time the flags were being waved for the 1977 Silver Jubilee, but something special was starting to blossom beneath the surface too.

Jago knew that the rough diamonds of Millwall's junior ranks that had been so expertly mined by Billy Neil required the attention of a fresh expert. Enter Oscar.

Luis Oscar Fulloné Arce – better known at the time as Oscar Arce – was appointed youth team coach for the 1977-78 season. It was an incredible coup by the club – and Jago. Argentinian Arce reportedly chose Cold Blow Lane over the opportunity to manage El Salvador at the 1977 CONCACAF Championship. His coaching methods would be music to the up-coming Millwall stars' ears.

Gone was the relentless running of pre-season training. Oscar wanted all of his players to be as good as he was – which was a mighty and nigh-on impossible ask. But he didn't demand it. He didn't shout, bully, humiliate, bellow constant reminders of how far short his students were falling of their pass mark like some ignorant P.E. teacher.

He caressed and cajoled it out of his players who hung on his every word. For a change of scene, the club trained at the Crystal Palace National Sports Centre.

While the first team used the Olympic-standard running track for sprints and the arena's pitch for practice matches, Arce's youth team would be in the inside hall honing their foot juggling skills – with tennis balls.

For many this was probably a fruitless exercise at first, but such was the enthusiasm and willingness to learn from Arce, every member of that team bought into it – and quickly improved as a result.

In his autobiography *Psycho Pat – Legend or Madman*, Pat Van Den Hauwe describes his south London upbringing:

"I went to a small kiddies' school in Bermondsey, then on to Deptford Park School where I started playing football and soon noticed a kid called David Mehmet. He used to do things with a tennis ball that older lads could not do with a football; he had amazing talent and could keep the ball up for hours. All he wanted to do was play for Millwall."

Goalkeepers were included in Oscar's innovative tennis ball sessions too, as Peter Gleasure remembers:

"Oscar was way, way before his time, what a fantastic coach. He'd have you doing keepie ups around the perimeter of the pitch and if you dropped the ball you had to go back and start again."

"When he coached me he used to stand behind me, with a wall in front and ricochet the tennis ball off the wall at different angles and say: 'if you can catch that ball you can catch a much bigger ball'."

It all sounds very rudimentary now, but not compared to what many other clubs were doing at the time where goalkeepers were often virtual spectators during technical training sessions.

Oscar Arce's influence was far-reaching, but sadly all too short-lived. In his fleeting spell at The Den he not only revolutionised the training methods but proved to be resourceful with it at a club where finances were always limited.

One morning before his latest session, he asked the groundsman to fetch him some timber and board. He quickly assembled a four by four base and started feverishly sawing four very rough but recognisable body and head shapes.

In a lightning-quick feat of creative magic that would have put Blue Peter's Noakes, Purves and Judd in the shade, by the time the players had arrived to begin their latest lesson, the casters from the large metal paladin bin had been removed and added to the base.

For the next months, Millwall's 13-strong youth squad were able to wheel out this portable 'wall' and spend 90 minute sessions honing their free kick technique, curling around it, smashing into it and fully testing Gleasure without any team member risking a ball in the face – or somewhere altogether more painful.

Once again Arce had turned training sessions into a joy. Not so impressed were the bin men who had to drag the disabled dustbin like a giant stunned R2D2 when it was time to collect the rubbish.

Arce's creativity knew no bounds. Pre-season training was based at Richardson Evans Memorial Playing Fields in Wimbledon. There had to be some running of course, but even this was done with a twist with future Olympic decathlon star Daley Thompson a regular guest on cross country and hill runs in Richmond Park.

Sessions quickly returned to the enjoyable short, quick passing and ball-juggling drills on the farthest pitch at Richardson Evans. At the end of one session, Arce began nonchalantly juggling the ball.

It would have been nothing unusual by then for the Millwall lads who were quickly learning – and falling in love with – Olé football. On this occasion however, Oscar continued to juggle the ball as he accompanied the players on the long walk back to the changing rooms.

Reaching the stepped entrance to the building, as various team members carefully placed down their equipment and took their places in the dressing room for a debrief, Arce continued to juggle the ball, up the steps, down the narrow corridor, through several doors before finally entering the changing room.

Still juggling, and having had total control of the ball without the merest hint of dropping it for well over 30 minutes, once every player had sat down he flicked it up and caught it behind his neck and with a beam shouted: "Heeeeeyyyyyy!"

On another occasion, Arce suddenly left a training session at The Den's adjacent New Cross Stadium and set off to a garage close to the Five Bells pub. Moments later he reappeared with ten Jaguar car tyres.

He then assembled the players on the dog track and lay the tyres down at various points with a ball beside them and instructed the players to 'tackle' them. Each squad member steamed into the large rubber opponent to win the ball.

Post-training nutrition for the first team at the time was a ham roll, cheese roll and cup of tea provided by the club tea lady Lil. Meanwhile Oscar Arce, Ian Gale and Phil Coleman would disappear in the club Dormobile and arrive back with 14 servings of fish and chips.

The 1977-78 season would see an unprecedented investment in the youth set up at Millwall, believed to be in the region of £30,000.

This was a no mean amount for a time when the club could seriously ponder investing half of that figure on a first team transfer fee. Footballing talent was in abundance right across London at the time.

QPR had arguably led the way and their embarrassment of riches had benefitted Millwall with Jago arriving from there to ply his trade at The Den, and with more of Rangers' forward-thinking, youth-focussed coaches on the way too - but under somewhat less fortunate circumstances which were, as is often the case with the club, lurking around the next corner.

Millwall's scouting network was laid out with almost military efficiency.

The M4 corridor was covered (which led to the recruitment of Slough-based Dean Horrix, among others) and in the opposite direction the A13 was also peppered with talent-spotters overseen by Bob Pearson. A conveyor belt of talent was being assembled at all levels from Under 16 through to Under 18. Players were confident in their ability, flourishing under the expert coaching of Oscar Arce, and toughened by the hourly Thursday sessions against the first team. It was a first team that, in the opening months of the new campaign had somewhat surprisingly failed to build on the progress and promise of the 76-77 season.

The worrying signals had been there from day one. Another south London team that was building a young side from local talent was Crystal Palace.

Millwall had gloriously pipped them to a Third Division promotion place in 1976 but they were back with a vengeance and took Millwall apart in a humiliating 3-0 first day Den defeat.

A heated argument between The Lions' Tony Hazell and goalkeeper Nicky Johns as they left the pitch did not bode well.

Blissfully unaware and happy to concentrate on their footballing education under Oscar Arce, Millwall's young players provided the club with an insurance policy and it was widely felt that this was no more than a blip, but everything was about to change irrevocably for the worst.

Millwall had always been a club troubled by football hooliganism, but it was never seen as that much more of a problem there than anywhere else and, as was common of the time, blamed on the exuberance of youth culture. That was until the television viewing nation sat down to watch popular current affairs programme Panorama on November 14th 1977.

It was a night that changed the path of Millwall Football Club forever.

Ordinary Boys

4

Fifteen Minutes of Infamy

These days it's not unusual to sit down in front of the television on any given evening and find, on one of the hundreds of channels available to us, a 'real life' or 'exposé' documentary that 'lifts the lid' on previously little-known topics.

They are mischief-making at best, attempting to attach labels to, or reinforce well-worn stereotypes about people who live on benefits or have inordinate amounts of offspring.

The thing is these days, most of the population has had so much of this drivel drip-fed to them they are either immune to it, or simply don't give it any credibility.

Social media provides the outlet for the faux outrage for the duration of the programme or perhaps for half an hour afterwards and maybe Piers Morgan will have one of his rants about it the following morning, but it is almost always completely forgotten within a day or so.

The television-viewing and newspaper-buying public of the 1970s however were a very different breed. Let's remind ourselves that in 1977 we had just three television channels to choose from and journalism was considered a far more respectable profession than it is today.

The popular and largely accurate perception back then was that our quality daily newspapers provided us with totally factual information – scandal was of course still rife but reserved for the tabloids and Sunday editions.

The pressure to sell newspapers was obviously there but nowhere near as intense as later years. Our television programmes carried even more credibility.

There were so few to choose from, how could you possibly doubt them? In 1977 it was pretty much the case that if a newspaper reported something on its front page it was treated as solid fact and believed.

Similarly, anything reported on the evening news was once again taken as read. Few members of the general public suspected a secret agenda or manipulation of the facts, and when it came to current affairs programmes and documentaries, the message was given even more credence.

Panorama is the BBC's multi award-winning flagship current affairs output and having first broadcast in

1953, is the world's longest-running news television programme.

In its early years it reflected the more innocent times that it broadcast in, and was famous for its 1957 April 1st edition which convinced the nation that spaghetti was grown on trees. It may have been intended as nothing more than a playful April Fools jape, but the reaction it received with many falling for it albeit temporarily, will have shown the programme makers just how much power and influence they potentially wielded.

Two examples of the topics it dealt with earlier in 1977 were investigating if the best days of your life really were at school and an interview with the then leader of the opposition and possible first ever female Prime Minister Margaret Thatcher.

In November of that year though it decided to broadcast a programme that will have had viewers scratching their heads in bewilderment at its title, but, as with the spaghetti spoof story two decades before, most were soon hanging on its every word.

'F Troop, Treatment and the Half-Way Line' was the title of the Panorama report broadcast on BBC1 on November 14th, 1977. The programme was introduced by a grim looking gentleman who warned of the upcoming bad language "that you wouldn't normally hear on television". With the title reinforced on a graphic behind the presenter showing a terrace of football supporters, we were informed that the piece would focus on "the terrace gangs that followed one small Second Division club: Millwall – in London's docklands".

Immediately the stage had been set. Millwall had been quickly set up as a 'small' football club – a fact that no fan would have disagreed with, but one that shouldn't really have been relevant to a programme apparently reporting on football hooliganism.

The problem was widespread throughout the country – especially in London – but had now also started to spread across Europe with English clubs' increased involvement and success in European competitions.

What followed was a 30-minute demonisation of an entire football club and its supporters. The objective was clearly to ensure this societal problem, which was commonplace in almost every town and city of the UK, was given a recognisable brand, to remove any ambiguity in the future and enable the authorities, media and any other organisation that wished to do so to divert the attention in another direction to suit their agenda.

They did it with Teddy Boys, Mods, Skinheads and punks and now they were doing it with football – and the ultimately disposable scapegoat they had chosen was Millwall Football Club.

It's not necessary to go into any detail about the programme. Most people are familiar with its content.

As some of the fans featured in it are no longer with us it's neither relevant nor respectful to do any more than remind you of the basic narrative. What's far more pertinent however is how far removed this was from what the BBC sold to Millwall Football Club when they sought their permission to have unprecedented access to the club and its staff.

Millwall were keen to show the initiatives that the club had put into place to try and curb the increase in terrace trouble. Measures that appeared to be working. The irony was that, whilst incidents across the country – especially London - seemed to be on the rise, arrests at Millwall matches in the two seasons that Gordon Jago had been in charge had fallen.

The club was trying revolutionary new stewarding procedures and other proactive, positive ideas rather than just burying its head in the sand or leaving it to the Police.

Fans were encouraged to spend more time at the club on non-match days, working on Sunday markets and other community events which gave them more of a sense of belonging and responsibility to help keep the club's good name.

Confident that such a respected broadcaster as the BBC would honour their intention to show the viewing public these forward-thinking attempts to solve the hooligan issue, they welcomed them into The Den. The result was catastrophic.

Hooliganism had, up until the broadcast of this programme, been a mostly generic, anonymous phenomenon. In less time than it takes to watch half a football match, they had given it an identity, a label and held it up almost as a challenge for every other football club in the country to do the same.

The club and local police reviewed the film but, despite voicing their disgust at the irresponsible, inaccurate and duplicitous nature of it, did not have the power of veto. For once, Millwall had the backing of the Police who, quite rightly felt that the programme didn't simply report on football hooliganism but glamorised and pretty much encouraged it.

A section of the programme was given over to a planned 'off' at the upcoming Spurs v Millwall match – which never actually materialised. It only served to reinforce allegations that those featured in the programme were actually paid up to £30 to appear in it and therefore, do as instructed.

They can't be blamed in any way. Give a few youngsters a few free beers and stick a television crew in front of the them and they are bound to perform. None of them can have imagined the fallout from their fifteen minutes of infamy.

It was a fallout that reached as far as The House of Commons and prompted Sports Minister Dennis

Howell to call an urgent meeting with Millwall officials and BBC Chairman Sir Michael Swann. Swann, unsurprisingly defended the programme but Howell was encouragingly on the side of The Lions as was evident in his statement following the broadcast:

"The general opinion is that it was the most irresponsible programme seen for a very long time…manufactured…doing a great disservice to football. What concerned us was the total lack of balance: apparently there was not one decent Millwall supporter they could find for the programme."

That last line really was the dagger to the heart of the club, given that the slot immediately following the piece which was intended to allow a discussion on the issues raised – and therefore allow Millwall a right of reply – was scrapped in favour of a last-minute special report on the Firemen's strike.

Whilst it was good to have both the Police and Sports Minister seemingly on side, the damage had of course been done.

Millions of people, many who probably had no knowledge of football at all and possibly only had knowledge of football hooliganism via fleeting glances in the daily newspaper, were now convinced that Millwall were the chief culprits and probably responsible for every act of football-related violence they saw in the daily editorials or news bulletins.

Not only that, but the disorganised rabbles that followed other clubs and enjoyed a few terrace fisticuffs every weekend would now have felt duty bound to sort themselves out, come up with names for their gangs and try to meet the challenge set down by Millwall.

But of course, it hadn't been set down by Millwall at all. Panorama had, just a few days after bonfire night, lit the blue touch paper and ran. They had declared war amongst football's fighting few and the promptly hid behind the sofa revelling in the chaos that they had initiated, Millwall meanwhile were left to clean up the mess. And what a mess it was.

Devastated, Jago must have felt partially responsible. He wasn't of course. His only failing was to trust what he thought was a globally respected broadcaster to be honest and faithful in producing a fair balanced account of what was going on. No-one at Millwall then – as today – pretended they were angels and denied there were any problems with the club's fans but, now, whenever an incident occurs, if it involves Millwall, the coverage it is given is always far more disproportionate than when it involves other clubs.

It is always "Millwall fans" involved in incidents, as opposed to "fans at an x v x match". That is the legacy of Panorama. It didn't just fade away. It hung in the air over The Den and cursed it for decades.

The club's response in the next match programme was immediate, understandably outraged and backed its fans:

"The Directors of Millwall Football Club whilst recognising that their Club, in common with other clubs throughout the Football League, suffer from a degree of hooliganism, consider that the BBC Panorama programme transmitted on Monday 14th November grossly exaggerated the size of the problem at Millwall. The number of hooligans at Millwall is estimated authoritatively to be less than 200 out of a loyal and responsible average home gate of approximately 10,000.

Whilst the Directors of Millwall are very conscious of the problem of hooliganism, and have taken, and are taking, active steps to combat the activities of a small number of persons, they consider that the Panorama programme as transmitted was an insult to the overwhelming majority of their supporters who are well-behaved, and that it conveyed an utterly false impression of the extent of the problem at Millwall, since the Club has recently enjoyed a good record of crowd behaviour as was underlined in the survey published in the Daily Mail and the Evening News on 14th November, and to which no reference was made in the programme. It was particularly unfor-

tunate that because of the late coverage given to the Firemen's Strike in Panorama, the BBC felt unable, despite prior assurance to the contrary, to give opportunity for comment in the programme itself, as the absence of such comment produced an unbalanced programme which will have conveyed a misleading impression to the general public. Moreover, by interviewing a limited and unrepresentative cross-section of people, and then concentrating the programme on such people, and by predicting violence at future matches, the BBC may well have succeeded in encouraging, rather than discouraging, unruly behaviour.

Whatever happens in the controversy now raging about the BBC Panorama programme on 14th November, your club directors are determined that the good name and reputation of the overwhelming majority of those who give their loyal support to Millwall F.C. is vigorously defended. Our official statement, which was carried in the press last week, shows clearly where we stand. No doubt you have all been following the developments in the press, on T.V. and radio since the programme was shown.

Many influential organisations and people have condemned the programme, not least the Football League, Football Association and the Minister of Sport, and revelations in the press that some of the participants in the programme may have been paid for taking part have helped to increase the general distaste created by the programme. Meanwhile, we at Millwall are taking advice on the best way of repairing the damage that the programme did to our club, but at this stage, the least said about these latest developments the better. Far more important is that we at Millwall, and that means directors, staff, players and supporters, retain the solidarity and confidence in each other that has brought this club through 92 years of existence, no matter how hard the going has been at times. AND THE TRUTH IS THAT IF IT WASN'T FOR OUR SUPPORTERS THERE WOULDN'T BE A MILLWALL FOOTBALL CLUB. Perhaps people not involved in the game do not realise what goes to make a Football League club; perhaps they cannot appreciate that without the deep and sincere involvement of the community, without a local loyalty that has its roots imbedded in the history of football, the running of a club these days would be impossible. It is essential, therefore, that the 99 per cent or more of our supporters, those whose support gives this club life and hope, are aware of the value which we place on their loyalty. Even those of the area who do not attend regularly feel that Millwall F.C. is part of their lives and we are encouraged by their interest. We know that what Millwall F.C. means to many thousands of people is not likely to be obliterated by the activities of a pitiful few. When the activities of that few are focused upon to the exclusion of all other aspects of a responsible and knowledgeable band of supporters, then an injustice has been committed, which could result in lasting damage to our club. We make no attempt to hide that a problem does exist, just as it exists at most of the 92 clubs in the Football League, but there are right and wrong ways of dealing with it and we know that our efforts were succeeding. When we visited Blackpool last week the local police added an extra 80 constables to their usual number on duty at the match. They did that, we were told because they had seen the Panorama programme. But there was not a single incident — needless to say this was not reported. This doesn't mean to say the problem has disappeared, but it does put it in perspective. Our task now is to see that the record is put straight and to work together to ensure that Millwall F.C. faces a proud and flourishing future."

In the summer of 1989, when Millwall were looking to attract a new commercial shirt sponsor to bring in much-needed revenue for squad-strengthening following their first ever season in Division One, director Peter Mead thought it would be a relatively simple task. Mead was, after all, a partner in Abbott, Mead and Vickers, one of the largest and most respected advertising agencies in the business.

However, after approaching every single one of his clients with the proposal of their brand appearing on the front of Millwall's shirts at Anfield, Highbury, White Hart Lane and Old Trafford, not only did all of them decline, but virtually every one sited the Panorama programme as their reason not to take the risk of their logo appearing on the front pages of the papers as part of a football riot report rather than the back.

Less than a month after the programme aired, and with its issues still being discussed in newspapers and on the radio, Gordon Jago quietly left his post as Millwall manager.

For the second home game running, Millwall fans had to read more bad news in the pages of their match day programme:

"The events of the past week have left us without a manager and, whilst the directors of Millwall neither expected nor wanted Gordon Jago to leave, we must now deal with the situation in which we find ourselves bearing in mind that at all times the Club is more important than any individual.

The Board's statement on Monday made it clear that they were unhappy the manager should want to leave with 18 months of his contract still to run. But once it became clear that he was set on starting a new career in the United States there was no point in Millwall standing in his way. Thus, he was released immediately. Now we look to Theo Foley, and the players to ensure that the club doesn't suffer in any way while consideration is being given to the question of Gordon Jago's successor. Thankfully, the team has shown a great improvement recently and last Saturday fought back from being 2-0 down at Oldham to gain a very creditable draw.

That is the spirit which has been evident in recent away matches and which will accelerate our progress during the rest of the season. Dwelling on the disappointment of Gordon's sudden departure will not help that progress but at the same time we cannot ignore what has been achieved in the three years in which he has been part of our long-term planning.

There are still problems to be solved but a great deal of important groundwork has been done and we are sure the new man can take us from strength to strength. Gordon Jago, himself certainly feels this way.

Before he left the club at the beginning of the week he said: "Whoever replaces me will find the foundations of success at Millwall and in many ways I envy him. Apart from the club's ambitions he will find an enjoyable setup here —it is certainly the most enjoyable club I've ever been associated with and this is because of its people. From the supporters, to the players and to the directors there is a close-knit feeling of pride and passion for the club and the game. After reading that I know people are going to ask why on earth I'm leaving. Well, I don't think anyone can understand what agony I've had in making my decision. In fact, I tried very hard to persuade the Tampa Bay club to delay my appointment until at least the end of the season. They made a fabulous offer but as far as I was concerned it came a year too soon. In a year's time I am sure that Millwall will be reaping the benefits of all our work over the past three years and, naturally, I wanted to be here to enjoy it. But the American job wouldn't wait, and I had to make the most difficult decision of my life. It was hard for me to ask the Millwall board for my release, particularly as the chairman has supported me wholeheartedly."

It was a statement that was every bit as bitter and wounded as the previous one had been defiant. The club clearly parted company with Jago as an immediate reaction to the Panorama programme, yet there was an attempt to suggest that interest from the US had been there all along.

It's hard to imagine Jago's transatlantic suitors being so insistent as to demand he resign immediately, half way through a league season.

It may well have been that attempts were made by all parties to see the 77-78 campaign out, but it's equally hard to imagine how Jago could have possibly continued to focus on coaching duties with him being such a central - if innocent - part of the whole mess.

The club had been travelling on a steady upward curve for over two years now, but suddenly it was to go into a nosedive.

Ordinary Boys

Out of the Frying Pan

The scars of Panorama would prove to be a lifelong blemish for Millwall Football Club. As 1978 arrived and the first team threw themselves into Second Division survival, the initial wound was allowed to partially heal before the scab was viciously ripped off and salt poured in.

Just weeks before his sudden and shocking departure, Jago had used his programme notes to heap praise on the now blossoming and rapidly progressing young Lions. They had started the season with a 4-2 win over the seemingly invincible Crystal Palace.

Palace were FA Youth Cup holders and on their way to back-to-back wins in the competition. The graduation process was beginning as players began to feature for Terry Venables' newly-promoted first team - the same one that brushed Millwall aside 3-0 at The Den on the same opening day. Palace were just ahead of Millwall's schedule it seemed, as Jago underlined in his notes, revealing that he'd probably like to have played many of them in his faltering first eleven:

"One only wishes they were 17-year-olds instead of 16. It is felt that this present team will provide the nucleus of the club's first team in the near future."

These weren't just empty words, and if any supporters were reading these notes and had even a passing knowledge of what was going on behind the scenes at Millwall, Palace and QPR, they should have had cause to be very excited and optimistic about The Lions' short term future.

There was something of a football talent triangle going on between Rangers, Millwall and Palace at the time. Jago had arrived from West London having witnessed the culmination of a brilliant crop of youngsters progressing into the first team that would continue into the eighties.

It was a revolutionary new coaching ethos that he had built on and brought with him to Millwall - leading to the appointment of Oscar Arce - and, all things being equal, Millwall could have expected to enjoy virtually guaranteed success at first team level in the coming seasons.

As Jago's first team struggled to build on the previous season's healthy showing, the youth team went from strength to strength and by October topped the South East Counties League Division One table unbeaten after beating Arsenal 3-2. In their wake were QPR,

Fulham and Crystal Palace, a feat made all the more remarkable when you consider four of the team were still aged just 15 and still at school.

It is interesting to note that Millwall's reserves also regularly saw five or six of the junior squad line up alongside or against out-of-favour or injury-recovering experienced professionals in the Midweek League.

A disappointing Youth League Cup exit at Palace was tempered by more scintillating league form with successive wins over Chelsea and West Ham and topped off by an FA Youth Cup first round 10-0 tonking of Maidstone where Chris Dibble bagged four goals, David Pearce a hat-trick and one each for Glen Morris, Morgan Evans and Phil Coleman.

Dibble was one player whose path to Millwall didn't follow the usual route.

Whilst others were courted by various clubs and chose Millwall for its unique appeal and persuasive skills of Bob Pearson, Chris Dibble arrived at The Den after fully expecting to become a Chelsea player – only for a mysterious involvement in crowd trouble to see him end up at The Den.

A regular on the Stamford Bridge terraces and established at the club as a schoolboy, Dibble was dumfounded to be told when he came to sign apprenticeship forms that, as the club records showed he had been involved in fan disturbances at the club, they would not be making the offer.

Dibble insists to this day that he has absolutely no recollection of any such incident!

Word soon got around that the promising young striker was without a club and within days Millwall manager Gordon Jago himself paid Dibble's home a visit.

"Gordon Jago came round to my little council house where I lived with my mum and dad and we couldn't believe what a nice bloke he was" recalls Dibble.

"He talked so well about Millwall and was such a gentleman my mum and dad were really impressed, then when I met Bob Pearson, I knew it was the right club."

By the time of Jago's departure, Millwall's reserves featured most of their youth squad, with the juniors blooding even more raw talent at schoolboy level.

It made for a slight blip in fortunes in the league, slipping to third behind QPR and Fulham, but was all part of the conveyor belt of talent that was chugging along nicely behind the scenes - even if there was turmoil at first team level.

A South East Counties League double was completed over Palace and progression to the fourth round of the FA Youth Cup achieved with a 4-1 replay win over Reading, meanwhile, victory over old foes West Ham saw them into the semi-finals of the Southern Junior Floodlit Cup courtesy of a Dave Mehmet penalty.

Mehmet, along with Dibble had long since made their first team debuts and perhaps the first signs of spreading the youth talent a little too thinly was evident in a shock FA Youth Cup fifth round exit at Grimsby. Overall though, things were looking brighter - even in the first team.

Respite from the unwelcome press attention and the rigours of keeping their tails away from the Division Three rat trap arrived in the shape of an FA Cup run which began with a Den replay win over Rotherham in January.

By then there was a new manager at the helm. George Petchey had taken over from caretaker Theo Foley. The change in personnel was, until Panorama, intended to come on the pitch rather than off it.

As part of his ambitious plans to play attractive football and following on from the influence of Argentinian youth team coach Oscar Arce, Gordon Jago had set up the exciting possibility of Argentinian stars Houseman, Babington and Fisher to come to The Den on loan spells.

The trio held Italian passports which would have enabled them to play in England under EEC laws. Of course, as Millwall learned with the infamous Russian loan duo of Yuran and Kulkov almost twenty years later, it wasn't a guarantee of success, but given Jago's

Midas touch, you'd have bet good money on that injection of talent benefitting the club. We'll never know, because that particular project evaporated as soon as Jago left.

A brilliant 4-0 home win over Luton saw them into the fifth round and a great chance of a place in the last eight of the competition when they were drawn at home again – this time to Notts County, but the two matches were sandwiched by a terrible tragedy that would put the club's rock bottom league position into very stark perspective.

A car carrying eight Millwall supporters to the league match at Southampton was involved in a collision with a lorry on the A33 near Winchester. John Webb, Stephen Bayes, Robert Bond, Stephen King, Stephen Medcraft, Rodney Phillips, William Ward and driver Arthur Smith were all killed in the tragic accident. The youngest was 19, the oldest 21.

The fifth round tie began with a poignant minute's silence and the laying of a wreath in the shape of an 8 on the pitch. The elation at reaching the quarter finals of the FA Cup for the first time in 41 years was understandably tempered by the tragedy that had preceded the 2-1 victory seven days before. Events that surrounded the last eight tie with Bobby Robson's

Ipswich three weeks later would plunge the club into further turmoil.

A bumper crowd of over 23,000 packed The Den to see if Petchey's relegation-haunted battlers could shock Robson's top flight title-challengers. They were given their answer just after 10 minutes when the visitor's full back George Burley put Ipswich in front.

By the time the final whistle sounded – some twenty minutes late due to a lengthy pause in play as police attempted to clear the pitch after fighting broke out on the terraces and spilled over the low perimeter wall – the match was long since over as a contest and the scoreline of 6-1 to Ipswich was an understandable side event to the main headline-grabber.

The club could not really point to the Panorama programme four months earlier as the catalyst for the disgraceful scenes that day, but there was no getting away from the fact that the programme had set Millwall's following as the standard-bearer for others hell bent on fighting at football.

You could argue that it exacerbated the problem but given the sheer nastiness of events that day – the game was briefly halted again in the second half to allow Ipswich goalkeeper Paul Cooper to clear broken bottles from his goalmouth – it was definitely a moot point.

The ultimate irony was of course that the match was covered by the BBC. The same BBC whose cameras the club had let in earlier that season under very false pretences and had now captured in theirs – and every non-Millwall supporter in the land's opinion – the ultimate justification of their Panorama programme. There was little Millwall Football Club could do or say in mitigation, they were well and truly painted into a corner and could only sit and wait for their punishment.

When it came it was another hammer blow that would drag the club further down into the mire:

The Millwall Football club shall, be closed for all matches from 26 March to 9th April inclusive.

For the coming two seasons all the matches of the Millwall FC in the Football Association Challenge Cup will be played on the ground of its opponents,

The sale of alcoholic drinks at the Millwall ground shall cease until further notice.

Fences, screens, barriers, or any other protection to be approved by the Football Association and other appropriate authorities shall be built before the start of next season.

In addition, the Millwall Football and Athletic Company Limited to be fined £1,500.

In making these decisions the Commission has taken into consideration the interests of opponent Clubs and the approaching end of the current season. The Commission reaffirms the views of other recent F.A. Commissions that as a first necessity steps should be taken to punish the hooligans responsible on these occasions. Unfortunately, this is not within the power of the Football Association and the Government must be pressed further into creating stronger deterrents and causing greater penalties to be laid down, legally enforceable, and applied.

The final paragraph of the statement was the killer. It was an admission that the best way to act after such an incident was obviously to punish the perpetrators, but that this was not possible so the entire club would be made to pay.

A sort of: "Look, we really hate doing this guys, but what choice do we have?". The Football Association now had the spotlight shone directly at it after such events. The whole country was watching unfold what the good old BBC had foretold a few months before and even those with not one scintilla of interest in the game, wanted to know what was going to be done about it. Politicians now had a brand new toy to play with and manipulate for their own interests.

Needless to say, it would take dozens more incidents met with a similarly ineffective punishment before the powers that be realised the only way to try and eradicate the problem was to actually punish the perpetrators, not the club they claim to support.

As one of the most tumultuous and damaging seasons in the club's long history drew to an equally hair-raising conclusion, the club was hurting, cut deeply by the events of 1977-78.

Thankfully the wound hadn't run so deep as to affect Oscar Arce's young Lions. An Easter tour of France saw them return with two trophies for best defence and best young player and it was straight into action with a brilliant Southern Junior Floodlit Cup semi-final win over Fulham at Craven Cottage.

Falling behind to a freak goal saw 'keeper Peter Gleasure make an uncharacteristic mistake when attempting to collect a speculative lobbed ball into the area. Dibble restored parity before half time and further goals from Gale and another from Dibble in the second half saw The Lions into the two-legged final against Ipswich.

Millwall travelled to Suffolk for the first match of the final and the tie looked to be heading for a 1-1 draw thanks to a goal from Mehmet but an injury time winner sent Ipswich down to The Den with a slight advantage.

It was almost three weeks before the second leg could be arranged and a Chris Dibble goal midway through the second half of the Friday night Den decider saw Millwall make it 2-2 overall and send the final into a tense period of extra time.

A long season which had seen many members of the squad take part in South East Counties League matches, the South East Counties League Cup, FA

Youth Cup, reserves Midweek League and help the first team's battle against relegation finally took its toll however when they lost the chance to lift the trophy to virtually the last kick of the game.

Incredibly, the side were expected to fulfil their league obligations less than 24 hours later with a trip to Gillingham where they found themselves understandably flagging, and four nil down at half time.

Rather than a heated pep-talk, Oscar Arce had some sage half time advice that actually got the club into trouble with the FA as Phil Coleman remembers:

"We didn't arrive home until midnight on the Friday after the Southern Junior Floodlit Cup defeat at The Den. The South East Counties League insisted that we play our fixture away against Gillingham the next day at 11am. We were all knackered and by half time we'd had a player sent off, I'd scored an own goal, we'd given away two penalties and we were 4-0 down."

"Oscar pulled us together at half time and said simply: 'Training. Keep-ball'. We knew exactly what that meant and for the second half our ten players stayed virtually in our own half and kept the ball."

"At one point I was playing one-twos around their centre forward from the goalline to Peter Gleasure our goalkeeper who was stood on the penalty spot. They couldn't get it off us, we kept the ball the whole half and the game finished 4-0.

"It was that embarrassing the referee ended up reporting us to the FA for not taking the game seriously, but it was up to the opposition to come and get the ball off us and they couldn't. We'd been taught Argentinian pass and move keep-ball."

The season came to end on a much-welcomed positive note all round. The first team managed their great escape and avoided relegation despite the spectre of the season's events still hanging heavily over them.

Oscar Arce's young Lions finished a creditable fourth in the South East Counties League - a best ever for the club - and was primed and raring to go for the new season. The invaluable experience they had gained from first team and reserve action would stand them in good stead to push on and improve even more, but they would have to do it without their beloved coach.

6

All Change

They say a swan's elegant outward appearance as it glides seemingly effortlessly across the water is betrayed by the furious activity beneath, its legs scrambling like out-of-control pistons pushing the wheels of a runaway steam train. At the start of the 1978-79 season, Millwall football club was doing a very good impression of this process – but in reverse.

Outwardly the place was in total disarray, a mess, both on the pitch and off it. Goalkeeper Nicky Johns had departed in the summer, but for nowhere near the £200,000 that the press had reported. In fact, it just about covered the £60,000 bill for stadium modifications – not to improve or extend The Den for more fans to watch their team, but in line with recommendations following the incidents of unrest in previous seasons.

It was money that could and should have been spent on vital new blood for a first team that was playing in the second tier of English football through sheer luck against all odds following the previous season's miracle escape.

To face a new season with arguably a weaker squad in a stronger division was chancing their arm beyond any reasonable hope and even the most optimistic of fans must have been expecting that come May, they would find themselves back in Division Three.

Behind the scenes however, things were ticking over nicely. Additions had been made to Millwall's youth squad and they were ready to face a new season of challenges, to come of age as no Millwall youth team had ever done before.

But they would do it without their mentor and coach who had arguably been the architect of their exciting brand of football that was, like the man who had appointed him, years ahead of its time: Oscar Arce.

The Argentinian coach left The Den in typical Millwall fashion and was replaced without so much as a 'goodbye', as winger Kevin O'Callaghan recalls:

"One minute Oscar was here, the next he was gone. We just came in for training one day and he wasn't there. David Payne was brought in to replace him. He was a decent enough coach but with all respect he didn't really have to do much with the team, we were already up and running". Payne himself is happy to admit that his first taste of coaching was a relatively straightforward one:

"They didn't need a lot of advice from me really, they were very, very on the ball. There were a lot of old heads on young shoulders. The main problem I had was getting the whole team together for a team talk because a couple of them were still at school."

Croydon-born Payne had enjoyed a good career at Crystal Palace. He joined as an apprentice and was part of the legendary Burt Head team that reached the First Division for the first time in the club's history in 1969. He left for Orient in 1973, where he played under George Petchey - who had been a coach and teammate at Palace. When his playing career ended in 1978, he joined Petchey once more at The Den. Arthur Rowe also made the same move from Palace to Orient - and was now helping the club in a scouting capacity, proving that despite their struggles, Millwall was attracting coaching as well as playing talent - both young and old.

Payne was cautiously optimistic about his team's chances of success. He knew he had a talented bunch but also knew what they were up against. The resources of Arsenal, Spurs and Chelsea, and the momentum of two-time FA Youth Cup winners Crystal Palace tempered his expectations for league performance, and FA Youth Cup success certainly wasn't on his mind:

"I thought if we finished in the top half of the league we'd done quite well, I was without a few players on Saturday matches because they were playing for the first team. Having Terry Long there really helped because I knew him from Palace and Orient but the biggest influence was Bob Pearson who pretty much put the team together. It was brilliant the way he went round to the players' mums and dads and persuaded them to sign."

The first Millwall programme of the new season for the clash with Newcastle offered just an eleven-word explanation for Arce's departure, informing Lions fans (most of whom were probably unaware of his existence or influence anyway) that he had accepted a job offer from Sheffield United.

Arce's legacy remained though, with the players he taught so diligently remaining true to the pure football message he put across. Payne equally embraced it, rather than being intent, as some more egotistical coaches might have been, to put his own stamp entirely on the team. It would prove to be a perfect blend with Payne's tutelage coming via such greats as Head, Rowe and Petchey, married with the south American swagger that Arce had built as a foundation.

Striker Alan McKenna recalls feeling the Oscar influence as soon as he arrived:

"I could run all day and I would battle and if you look at a lot of the English teams at the time they all had a Scotsman in them. When I arrived at Millwall, I was aware straight away how much better the first touch was, and how the ball was always on the ground. I realised fairly quickly you have to improve your first touch so I worked on that and became a better player."

He also quickly recognised Payne's different, but equally influential coaching skills:

"David Payne was absolutely brilliant. If he had a favourite he never ever showed it." He recalls. He also remembers how Payne instilled some vital discipline in the team and how, on the rare occasions it was needed, let a bunch of very confident and head-strong players know exactly who was in charge:

"I remember one day, we were training on the RedGra pitch behind The Den, we were doing a lot of running, really getting our arses tanned that day. On the way back Paul Roberts was niggling Payney. He was told a couple of times to shut his mouth but he just wouldn't. We'd got to about fifty yards from the back door at the club and Payney stopped us and said:

'right, about turn, we're going back' and we went back for more."

Meanwhile, the first team had started the season brightly. The 2-0 victory over The Magpies provided hope, but it was an empty one. George Petchey's side wouldn't collect maximum league points for another three months.

Youth starlet Dave Mehmet was by now a regular in the side and it could have been argued that playing a 16-year-old in a side that was being mercilessly battered to certain relegation could prove to be a morale-sapping experience from which he might not recover.

Not that Mehmet was complaining:

"I wasn't the brightest kid at school if I'm honest, I got expelled from two. I grew up in Deptford, literally across the road from Millwall. I lived on the Pepys Estate and everyone there met up on a Sunday to play."

"My dad did a deal with he school where I'd go in and get my mark and then go and train with Millwall. It kept me out of trouble, kept me off the streets!".

"I just wanted to play football. I didn't care if it was for the youths, reserves or first team, and the rest of the lads were the same. You could be playing three or even four times a week sometimes, but we didn't care."

"The thing is training with Oscar was different, we trained three times a day but it was all ball work, no running. The first team used to want to train with us instead."

Phil Coleman and goalkeeper Peter Gleasure were the latest to sign full time professional forms as the season got under way. They were joined by ten new apprentices: Tony Kinsella, Tony Dark, Paul Roberts, Alan McKenna, Kevin O'Callaghan, John Helps, Andy Massey, Dean Horrix, Paul Robinson and Dave Martin. Their journey that season would be stratospheric. Tony Kinsella's footballing education began with future pros Paul Allen and Tony Mahoney. The skilful midfielder was certainly in demand, starting out at Fulham just as Mahoney was breaking into The Cottagers' first team and also training with Arsenal and Tottenham.

It was another feather in the irrepressible Bob Pearson's cap to persuade Kinsella to choose Millwall, making his approach via the youngster's school headmaster.

"Bob was phenomenal" Kinsella recalls. "My dad worked shifts at Ford and Bob used to pick me up and take me to games; he made regular visits to my house and sold the club to Mum and Dad."

"There were other clubs interested in me at the time and Paul Allen – along with his dad and uncle Les –

tried to persuade me to join him at West Ham, but Bob sold the club to us."

"When Bob Pearson started putting that team together you could see straight away there was something special there. We were turning over your Arsenals and your Tottenhams and you could tell we really had something."

Kinsella was another to benefit from Oscar Arce's coaching:

"He just seemed miles ahead of any other coach I'd ever worked with. Oscar taught me stuff that I kept throughout my career. He'd pull me to one side and explain what I was doing, what I wasn't doing and what I should be doing, it was a great learning curve for me. He helped to develop me into a player I really wanted to be."

By October Millwall's South East Counties League campaign had got off to a steady start with the team positioned nicely in fifth spot but with the struggles continuing in George Petchey's first team, more of the squad were being called upon to help the rock bottom Second Division strugglers.

David Gregory and Ian Gale joined Dave Mehmet in the first team with the pair being ever present throughout the month. Whilst it wasn't enough to improve the first team's fortunes, it certainly didn't detract from the youth side's progress as they racked up wins over Fulham and Arsenal, battered Colchester

9-0 and eased into the third round of the South East Counties League Cup 3-1 again against Arsenal.

They also went into November in third place in the league, just a point behind leaders Gillingham and Arsenal.

November continued in the same vein with league wins over QPR and Charlton. Goals were being spread liberally around the team with Coleman, Dibble, Gale and Edinburgh-born Alan McKenna contributing.

McKenna was the exception to the rule as far as Millwall's recruitment net coverage was concerned and once again it was down to Chief Scout Pearson that the Scottish striker decided to choose the blue and white of Millwall over that of Glasgow giants Rangers.

McKenna was on the Ibrox Club's books and also appearing for Scotland schoolboys and it was his performance for them against England at Wembley that alerted Pearson, who was a spectator that day.

McKenna felt that he was being messed about by Rangers and word reach Pearson who acted quickly. He arranged for the striker to appear in a trial match at Stoke Poges and invited George Petchey along to watch. He scored two goals and Petchey's immediate post-match reaction was "sign him", and McKenna swiftly crossed the border to sign for The Lions.

It would have been a huge step for a kid barely out of school to move almost 400 miles from home and share the same Dulwich digs with Peter Gleasure and Dean Horrix - especially when his teammates were able to pop back home whenever they wanted to. It was testimony to both the team spirit and the mental strength of McKenna that he not only coped with it, but thrived.

Being part of the Millwall family certainly helped and McKenna was soon to discover exactly what this meant.

One evening he was approached in the old Den's Jubilee Bar by fan Ted Lynch. He introduced himself as a Millwall supporter, and, knowing that he was a young lad a long way from home, invited Alan to join him and his family for dinner.

McKenna was understandably a little apprehensive at first and politely declined but Ted kept the invitation open and eventually he accepted and joined Ted, his wife Eve and their two sons Danny and Tony for a meal. Not only did it become a regular occurrence with Alan also having a kickabout with the boys, no doubt providing McKenna with some vital friendship to help him to settle, they became life long friends and are still in touch today.

Victory over Spurs and then leaders Gillingham saw The Lions hit the top of the league going into December - sandwiched by a very routine 3-0 win at home to Slough Town in the second round of the FA Youth Cup, where Coleman, O'Callaghan and

Horrix were on target. O'Callaghan was the latest young Lion to catch the eye. The pacey, skilful winger earned selection for an England Youth XI and would later go on to earn full International honours - but not for England.

Gillingham were beaten again - this time in the second round of the Southern Junior Floodlit Cup and a 3-1 victory at home to Southend made it an incredible eleven match winning run with 32 goals scored and just five conceded. The new apprentices certainly seemed to be having an effect with Kinsella, Massey, Horrix and co all slotting in as if they'd been playing there for years.

If Millwall fans wanted a tantalising glimpse into the possible future for the club, they only had to look at the current Second Division league table as 1978 drew to a close.

At one end it made for painful reading with The Lions sitting second from bottom. Equally painful would have been the sight of rivals Crystal Palace top with a five point promotion cushion over fourth placed Brighton. Just three seasons earlier Gordon Jago's rampant Lions had pipped both Palace and Alan Mullery's Brighton to promotion to the Second Division and then looked a good bet to continue their upward progress before it had all come crashing down.

The silver lining was of course that both Palace and Brighton had surged on thanks to a wealth of youth talent which was now gradually blossoming in the first team and would go on to grace the top flight just months later. Millwall, it was felt (and not just by those at the club) had a youth team possibly far better than both, who were just 18 months to two years behind. Surely, if Petchey could just work his magic for one more season and keep Millwall in the second tier, the future was rosy?

The year ended with the long winning sequence coming to a stuttering halt with defeat to QPR and draws against Portsmouth and Arsenal but as 1979 began, all thoughts turned to the next round of the FA Youth Cup and Norwich at home in the third round.

It proved to be a routine win, almost matching the 4-0 victory away to the Norfolk side at the start of the season, with goals from Dibble, McKenna and O'Callaghan sealing a 3-0 passage into round four where they would face Sunderland.

It was a Norwich team that included a certain Justin Fashanu who was kept quiet by a strong performance at left back from Paul Robinson, who remembers the tussle well: "I had a real battle with Fashanu, I'd kicked him a few times and at one point we came together and nearly went through the big railings at The Cold Blow Lane end."

Palace meanwhile, who were hoping for a hat-trick of FA Youth Cups, took league points off The Lions when they recovered from a first half Horrix goal to beat The Lions 2-1. At the start of the season very little thought had been given to the FA Youth Cup, it really was just another game for Payne's hungry young Lions. Now however there was the realisation in the camp that, if they could get past Sunderland, they'd be just two ties away from the final - and stealing the crown from the Palace.

Ordinary Boys

7

"Mr Clough to You..."

Worryingly Millwall would go into their FA Youth Cup last sixteen clash with Sunderland on the back of their first bit of bad form all season. Back to back 0-2 defeats away at West Ham in the Southern Junior Floodlit Cup and at home to Chelsea in the league were a direct result of a bug sweeping through the squad which deprived them of Kevin O'Callaghan and Ian Gale.

Not that a small blip like that was going to knock their confidence - especially playing at The Den. The same bug saw Dave Mehmet only manage to figure in the first thirty minutes but The Lions emerged victorious from the tight tussle as 2-1 victors thanks to goals from Phil Coleman and Dean Horrix.

It was the first time Millwall had been really tested in the competition so far, and it would stand them in good stead for the battle that lay ahead. Meanwhile in the first team, manager George Petchey was struggling to lift his side for another great escape. A creditable goalless draw away to promotion-chasing Crystal Palace was followed by a brilliant 2-0 win away to relegation rivals Sheffield United, only for them to undo all that good work with a numbing 1-0 Den defeat to Sunderland - on the day that the matchday programme revealed the latest chapter in the youth team's FA Youth Cup charge in beating the same team to earn a place against Nottingham Forest or Portsmouth in the quarter finals.

The Lions were now five points adrift of safety. With two points for a win and games running out fast the future for the first team was looking considerably bleaker than for David Payne's youngsters.

Now back up to full fitness, they eased past Tottenham in the South East Counties League Cup semi final, lining up and end of season final with West Ham.

As Millwall fans faced up to the prospect of another nail-biting end to the season to see if their beloved Lions could hold on to their second tier status, they turned up at The Den to see if they could start by taking points off promotion-chasing Notts County.

Those who purchased a programme must have been incredulous to read the news on page three of that day's edition, which revealed a £10 million scheme had been approved to completely redevelop The Den and surrounding area.

The project - which apparently had been discussed for the previous three years - would include an internationally-sized ice skating rink, sports hall, squash courts, two cinemas, a 750-capacity club and lounge bar plus a multi-storey car park for 730 cars.

In addition, the project, which was a joint venture with Associated Dairies Group (ASDA) would see The Den completely revamped as a 25,000 capacity all-seater stadium.

It would be the start of a saga that would rumble on unfinished for years to come and provide nothing more than an irritating distraction to the continued decay occurring on the pitch.

Millwall fans weren't interested in an internationally-sized ice skating rink or turning The Den into a soulless all-seat arena. They just wanted their team to stay up, which was looking even less likely after another 0-1 home defeat to Notts County.

Two days after County left SE16 with both points, their Nottingham rivals Forest arrived, having despatched Portsmouth in their fourth round FA Youth Cup match. This would prove to be - as you'd expect in the last eight of a national cup competition - to be Millwall's sternest test yet. The match was also shrouded in sadness however. Two days later, The Den would be hosting a testimonial match for club secretary Gordon Borland. England manager Ron Greenwood - who was friends with George Petchey - had agreed to bring a young England team to play against a Millwall eleven. The match was to recognise a lifelong club servant whose loyalty had not gone unnoticed elsewhere. He had earlier received the Football Association's long service award in recognition for his time at his beloved Millwall where he had started out as personal assistant to Charlie Hewitt back in 1955.

Borland was a passionate believer in youth football at Millwall and an avid follower and supporter of the young Lions' fortunes. He'd also proved his worth to the first team in helping them achieve one of their great FA Cup giant-killing feats.

In 1973, before Millwall's away FA Cup fourth round tie at First Division Everton, he used a trip to in-laws who lived close to Goodison Park to attend one of the Merseysider's home matches and compile a detailed dossier for Benny Fenton. The information proved worthwhile as goals from Cripps and Wood gave Millwall a famous 2-0 win.

The club had announced the testimonial game at the start of March. Less than a week later, Borland died after being ill for some time. The testimonial became a tribute and Millwall's young Lions had even more incentive to extend their FA Youth Cup adventure. If they ever needed it.

Obviously success in the first team doesn't always mean the same at youth level - and vice versa as Millwall were currently proving.

However, with Brian Clough at the helm at Forest, ably assisted by Peter Taylor, these were heady days for the east midlanders and their mix of carefully-selected seasoned pros, rough diamonds and exciting youngsters had seen them win the First Division title and League Cup the previous season.

On their way to the first of their back-to-back European Cup triumphs, this kind of success couldn't fail to permeate down through the ranks as the club strived for continuity to build a footballing legacy.

Clough was already well on his way to achieving his legendary managerial status and made no secret that he took an interest in all aspects of the club - including the youth team.

With Millwall's own youngsters now catching the eye on a national stage as they moved into the latter stages of the competition, it was agreed that whichever team emerged victorious from this mouth-watering clash would almost certainly go on to be crowned FA Youth Cup winners.

The Monday night encounter got off to the worst possible start when Forest were awarded an early penalty which they duly despatched. Millwall fought back and on the stroke of half time were rewarded when striker Alan McKenna scored a deserved leveller.

The Lions came out firing in the second half and a brilliant right-foot strike from the edge of the area from Kevin O'Callaghan sent them into the lead and another from McKenna - heading home after more great work from O'Callaghan - looked to have finished the tie off and sealed their semi final place.

With twenty minutes to go however Forest found themselves right back in it thanks to a spectacular long-range shot which gave goalkeeper Peter Gleasure no chance.

Moments later the unthinkable happened when an almighty goalmouth scramble ended up with the ball in Gleasure's net once more as the leg-weary Lions appeared to be running out of steam - and going out of the cup.

It was to their immense credit that they resisted what looked like an inevitable Forest winner but they must have nevertheless been devastated at the final whistle to know they would have to do it all again in a replay at The City Ground after seemingly having the tie in the bag.

If the loyal Lions followers who witnessed that incredible match had doubts that Payne's battle-weary warriors could reproduce another equally gutsy performance in the replay, they weren't shared by the players.

After the match, Forest winger Steve Burke struck up a bet with Millwall defender Dave Martin. Burke bet £50 that they would "smash them" in the replay at The City Ground. Martin happily accepted the challenge.

It was raining goals in the league too. The Forest goal-fest was sandwiched by another 3-3 - this time at Spurs, a 2-2 away to Orient, and a 3-2 win at Chelsea - all in the league to send Millwall up to third place.

Horrix was starting to get amongst the goals more and more and grabbed two against Chelsea as The Lions recovered from a 1-2 half time deficit but his season as about to take a much darker turn when he took his place on the bench at Forest for the replay.

Unlike the first encounter, the rematch was tourniquet tight from the first whistle with neither side as keen to over-stretch themselves or take any risks.

The breakthrough came for Millwall however when Tony Kinsella gave The Lions the lead.

It's a goal that Kinsella recalls particularly well:

"After the draw at The Den the Forest players clearly felt they were favourites to win the replay and get into the semi-finals but we went up there and I scored I think the only goal I've ever scored with my right foot."

Keen to freshen legs and not sit back, striker Horrix was brought on from the subs bench.

Less than ten minutes after joining the action however, he was involved in an horrific clash and had to be stretchered off with what first appeared to be serious facial injuries.

In typical fashion for that band of brothers, they appeared to be galvanised rather than depleted by the loss of one of their own to such a shocking injury, and despite Nottingham Forest throwing everything at them for the rest of the match, produced a defensive display way beyond their years to grind out a famous 1-0 victory.

Breathless and bloodied, they returned to the dressing room to celebrate one of the club's most remarkable feats at that level.

It would later transpire that Horrix had in fact suffered two hairline fractures to his skull, but mercifully no permanent eye damage as had first been feared.

Millwall's young upstarts had defeated the youth team of what was, at that time, footballing royalty. All it needed now was a visit from the main man himself: Brian Clough. What would the chances of that be?

Giddy with the realisation of what he and his team had achieved, young captain Paul Roberts treated his colleagues to an impromptu impression of how he thought Clough might have reacted to seeing his team defeated on their own turf.

At that time, millions were tuning in to enjoy impersonator Mike Yarwood - who had made the Forest manager one of his signature take-offs.

Just as Roberts was in full flow, he was oblivious to the dressing room door opening and a figure in an unmistakable green jersey appearing at it. It was Brian Clough. He had decided to pay the young Lions a visit to congratulate them on their performance and wish them well in the semi-final.

Clearly unimpressed by Roberts' efforts, after a brief rebuke (a look was usually enough from him) he offered his congratulations to the team and turned to leave.

"Yeah nice one, cheers Cloughie" came the response from Roberts, complete with a thumbs-up.

Clough span round to face the young defender and, with his face bright red with fresh rage, boomed:

"IT'S MR CLOUGH TO YOU!"

As comical as the incident was, it was enough to compel the Nottingham Forest manager to make a complaint to the club and the squad returned to south London to a ticking off from first team manager George Petchey - but it must have been done with a barely-disguised wry smile at the corner of the mouth. At a time when Cloughie was appearing on peak-time chat shows and throwing down challenges to Muhammad

Ali, he had crossed swords with little old Millwall and finally met his match. Although Steve Burke never did pay out on that bet.

Funnily enough, it wouldn't be the last time a young Millwall defender impersonated him. Almost ten years later, while recording a commemorative Christmas video for sale in the club shop, Neil Ruddock could be seen giving Teddy Sheringham a Cloughie lecture, ironic of course that just two years after Sheringham would sign for Forest and play under the famous manager.

A 1-4 defeat to Southend when the team were required to return to South East Counties League action just 48 hours after returning from Nottingham was understandable - especially with the first leg of the semi final to come just four days after that.

Millwall's squad was in no doubt that the two-legged format of both semi-final and final (should they reach it, which by now they were confident they would now) would be hugely in their favour.

There was little doubt that their campaign that season had been boosted by home draws and whilst The Den wasn't quite as intimidating with only a few hundred hardy souls cheering The Lions on, it wasn't just the terraces that provided an daunting welcome to visiting teams.

As Eamon Dunphy described in his book "Only A Game?", as a visiting player arriving at The Den for his then club York City, every aspect of the matchday experience was foreboding. From the dark, tunnelled approach to the stadium to the dank, depressing changing rooms in the bowels of the main stand with it's leaking taps and faulty light bulb. Can you imagine being a youngster arriving for a night match to that? If anything, the dark, shadowy, echoing, empty terraces would only have served to make the experience all the more chilling and oppressive.

By the time Forest came, the imagination had been captured and fans were turning up to see this fine young team of hungry new players that would surely mean a turnround in the fortunes of the first team soon and as any old Den regular will testify, even a couple of thousand in that old arena could make itself sound like twenty thousand.

Millwall's attempt to win the most prestigious prize in youth football would now move on to a much bigger stage: Merseyside. A first leg match at Goodison was the first hurdle they had to overcome, before taking on an Everton side containing such future stars as Kevin Ratcliffe, Steve McMahon and Joe McBride back to The Den where, all being well in that first leg, they would finish the job and take their place in the final.

Ordinary Boys

8

Boys to Men

By April Kevin O'Callaghan was a regular in the Millwall first team. Still six months shy of his eighteenth birthday, the responsibility of helping The Lions perform their second consecutive miraculous escape from the clutches of Division Three was being placed equally on his and fellow youth-team stars David Gregory, Chris Dibble and Dave Mehmet's shoulders.

As beleaguered boss George Petchey had previously alluded to, he would have no doubt utilised more of David Payne's FA Youth Cup semi-finalists had they not been of even more tender years. Paul Roberts was skippering the team at just 16 and playing, like his peers, at a level of footballing maturity way beyond what any coach could have realistically expected of them.

For a brief spell, it seemed that the success of the young Lions was having a positive effect on their first team counterparts and April blossomed for both as wins at home to Leicester, Orient and Cambridge raised hopes of escaping the dreaded drop.

In fact, by the time another point was gained in a 0-0 draw at home to Fulham on the eve of the eagerly-anticipated semi-final second leg with Everton, the first team were boasting their best run of the season with just one defeat in the last seven games and Mehmet on the scoresheet in consecutive matches.

Unfortunately for Petchey, Millwall's relegation rivals had also decided to make a late dash for safety and despite the brave run The Lions still found themselves second from bottom and five points adrift - just as they had been for what seemed like all season.

The youngsters however were just getting started.

Typically unfazed by a grand old stadium such as Goodison, (where 'keeper Peter Gleasure recalls his dad's amazement at there being a lift up to the directors box where supporters watched the match) Millwall had comfortably held Everton at bay and returned to London with a priceless 0-0 draw.

They would have a full eight days before facing West Ham in the South East Counties League Cup final first leg - but of course with some on first team duty, that wouldn't exactly be a rest.

And so it was, just twenty four hours after Gregory, O'Callaghan, Mehmet and Dibble had played ninety minutes for the first team in that draw with Fulham, they were back on The Den pitch, hoping to secure a place in a major final for the first time in the club's history.

A Den crowd that was every bit as raucous as the one that had been willing the first team on for survival the previous night were treated to a virtuoso display from the talented young Lions as goals from McKenna and Dibble eased them to a thoroughly professional victory over Everton who could have no complaints. They had been second best in both games, and Millwall were deservedly in the final.

A harsh winter had seen several postponements so as Payne's youth team started preparations for their two-legged final, Petchey's first team were at the last chance saloon in a season that was being extended well into May.

Needing nine points from their last five games to guarantee staying up (with just two points for a win) the survival bid started steadily enough with a 1-0 win away to Burnley, but crashed badly back in the north west with a crushing 1-4 defeat at Oldham. Millwall had literally hit rick bottom, they were 22nd in the Second Division table and all but relegated.

There was brief respite and the joy of putting one over their old foes with a midweek 2-1 win at The Den against West Ham in front of a surprisingly low crowd of less than 12,000. The win was secured with another goal from Mehmet - just 48 hours before he was due to line up with his youth team colleagues for the first leg of the final at Maine Road. The next day the team travelled to Manchester - but without one of their teammates.

Paul Robinson was the second youngest in the team and, like the youngest - Dave Martin - was still at school. In fact, on the day of the first leg of the final, instead of being at the hotel with the rest of the team, he was sitting a French exam back in London.

As soon as it was finished, a car was sent by the club to collect him from the school gates and drive him to Euston station where he boarded the train for Manchester Piccadilly. There another car collected him and dropped him at Maine Road stadium in time for kick-off.

Hardly the best of preparations, and that wasn't the only glitch in the build-up to the back night.

At the start of every season, each full-time professional on Millwall's books received a sheet of paper detailing their various bonuses for the up-coming season. The devil in the detail on this priceless ledger was how much cold hard cash each player received for an appearance in the various teams, goals scored, competitions won etc.

There was an omission from the bonus sheet for Millwall's youth team for the 1978-79 season that went unnoticed it seemed by every member of the squad. It'd be impressive to say that, so focussed were they on the business of winning football matches that they didn't care for such monetary carrots. It would also be untrue. First team regulars let alone newly-signed teenage pros were of course not banking the ridiculous riches they do today and so relied on the extra few quid that a win or a goal would garner. The ultimate payday however for any full time professional footballer would be winning the ultimate competition – the FA Cup. This would be up there bonus-wise with getting your eight from ten score draws on a good week on the pools. Highly unlikely, but hugely lucrative.

Whilst the youth version of the competition was never going to be on anywhere near as grand a scale or financially beneficial for the club that won it, previous winners had proved it to be an exciting barometer for future success – as Crystal Palace were now proving.

It would be fair to assume then that when Millwall's young Lions scanned their bonus sheet that summer, all eyes would be on what was on offer were they to finish the season as FA Youth Cup winners.

Apparently not!

Captain Paul Roberts recalls the moment it dawned on the squad that any reward for winning the biggest competition in the youth game had not been agreed. It was the day of the final:

"I was stood on the steps to the hotel we were staying at in Manchester on the day of the first leg of the final at Man City. I was watching Dave Mehmet who was, as usual, juggling a ball around the grass at the front of the hotel. Suddenly he stopped, picked up the ball and walked over to me."

A light bulb had suddenly gone off in the talented young midfielder's usually football-dominated brain.

"He asked me what bonuses we'd be getting if we won the FA Youth Cup" Roberts recalls.

Mehmet had spent much of that season playing for the youth team one week and the first team the next. Few players at the club could have had opportunity for a better understanding of the mechanics of Millwall Football Club's player admin from the top to the bottom. He'd have been rubbing shoulders and sharing communal baths with wizened old pros who had decades of experience in extracting the minutiae of every penny owed to them for every possible positive outcome from this mad game. They wouldn't have had agents to do such dirty work and whilst they almost certainly would have been very secretive about any personal details, it would surely have been impossible for Mehmet to miss a trick?

But miss it he had, as had the rest of the squad.

"I didn't know" admitted Roberts. "To be honest, none of us really thought about it, we just went out there and played".

It wasn't quite the altruistic approach I'd thrown out there earlier, but nevertheless, in their quest to out-football all before them and beat everyone, this rather crucial detail had slipped the net and needed to be rectified immediately. For the first time, something took precedence over the football and Roberts was now at the centre of it.

"We got the players together and decided we needed to know what our bonus would be if we won the FA Youth Cup. The only way to do that was to speak to the directors. As club captain the rest of the team agreed that was my job and that I'd have to phone him straight away, from the hotel. I was still only 17 and didn't know where to start."

The club director in charge of such matters at the time was Herbert Burnige, a Mr Millwall if ever one existed. By all accounts a kindly, affable and friendly custodian of the club he loved. Certainly not in the mould of some of the tyrants that ruled the boardrooms elsewhere in the game, no Deadly Doug by any stretch, and yet still, understandably the prospect of calling him to basically ask "What's in it for us?" as it felt to Roberts, must have been a daunting prospect, but call him he did:

"I went to reception and asked to use the phone to call Mr Burnige at the club. I was hoping I could just tell the lads that I'd called but he wasn't there. But by the time I'd put the receiver to my ear and turned around, all the boys were in reception with me listening in to what was happening."

"He was very good about it actually. He apologised for it not being sorted and said that this wasn't really the time to discuss it but that, if we won it, there would certainly be a bonus."

Any fear that might detract from the players' performance that evening at Maine Road were soon dispelled when they produced another well organised defensive display and held a Manchester City team including such future young stars as Alex Williams, Tommy Caton and Steve Kinsey to a goalless draw with some considerable comfort.

Whilst it wasn't in the nature of the team to be over-confident, especially as City's path to the final had come via victories on the road at Oldham, holders Crystal Palace, Luton and Southampton, they knew now exactly what they had to do, which was what they had been doing all season: win at The Den.

The Class of '79

The official listed attendance for Millwall versus Manchester City in the 1979 FA Youth Cup final second leg is 5,653. Anyone who was there on the evening of May 21st 1979 will swear it was triple that but, such was the power of The Den, the atmosphere and noise generated could often sound like twice the actual crowd. Either way, Millwall fans turned up in their numbers to see if their talented crop of young Lions could finish the job that had started back in November with a routine victory over Slough Town.

In reality of course it started long before then. The seeds of this blossoming side had been sown by the likes of Bob Pearson, Billy Neil and Oscar Arce two or three years before, but 1979 was the year they truly came of age, and now was their time. The cup run had been built on home success - as had many of the senior team's triumphs throughout the club's history. It was ironic then that, as the fans took their places on the terraces and in the stand, they did so once again as Third Division football fans - thanks mainly to the first team's failings at home.

The Division Two campaign still wasn't over - not as far as fulfilling fixtures was concerned at least - but for Millwall it had ended with failure to beat Fulham, a crushing 0-3 defeat to Bristol Rovers and a 2-2 draw with Wrexham, all at their beloved Den which was usually a fortress. Four points squandered that would have meant safety - at the expense of local rivals Charlton who had escaped the drop by a single point over Sheffield United and three clear of second-bottom Millwall.

Throughout the ill-fated campaign, first team responsibility had often fallen on the shoulders of several of The Lions' youth team who were battling their own campaigns on three other fronts apart from their FA Youth Cup challenge.

Always close to the top places in the South East Counties League table, as well as good campaigns in the South East Counties League Cup and Southern Junior Floodlit Cup - where they also reached the final - along with Midweek league appearances for many of the squad to boot meant the added distraction of first team football should have left them well and truly burnt out by the time the referee blew his whistle for the final ninety minutes of the final to begin. But far from burnt out, Millwall were absolutely blazing.

After dominating a first half where Mehmet hit the bar and McKenna saw several chances go begging the sides went into half time still deadlocked at 0-0 after 135 minutes of football. It didn't take long for that to change however, and typically Mehmet was involved.

His teasing free-kick in the first minute of the second period was turned into his own goal by a Manchester City defender and the lid was finally off as City had no reply for Millwall's attacking onslaught - let alone enough nous to unlock the impregnable defence so superbly marshalled by Phil Coleman and Paul Roberts. Just before the hour mark a left wing corner was met by an unmarked Coleman who powered a header past the despairing Williams in the City goal. At the other end, Millwall 'keeper Peter Gleasure had to wait until the 82nd minute before having anything to do. Then it was all over, they had done it.

The apparent ease with which Millwall beat Manchester City should not take anything away from their achievement.

The previous two seasons had seen a virtually unstoppable Crystal Palace team win the competition, the difference being the upward curve that the rest of the Selhurst Park club was enjoying.

Palace had relinquished their FA Youth Cup crown, but had moved on to bigger and better things. The triumphant members of those back-to-back final wins had just played their part in Palace winning the Second Division title and would be playing their football in the First Division next season.

The same should have been said of Millwall. Life is full of what-ifs, but there can be no doubt that had Jago not been forced to leave 18 months before in the wake of the Panorama fiasco, the club would have surely remained on a far smoother footing and been able to provide a settled, mid to top half of the table Second Division squad for the likes of Gleasure, Roberts, Coleman, Gregory, Dibble, McKenna, Massey and O'Callaghan to be eased into.

Meanwhile, a continued mining of the rich seam of footballing talent that was being so expertly scouted by Pearson and his colleagues could have continued, ensuring the future was well and truly secure. As it was, despite the euphoria of the win and another successful season for the Millwall Youth team, as the Champagne bubbles started to fade, the grim reality began to dawn on the club.

Twenty four hours after the young guns had lifted the FA Youth Cup, Millwall's first team made their apologetic bow from Division Two football with a feeble 0-2 defeat at home to Preston in front of a woeful attendance of 2,833 - a club record low league attendance. The line-up was once again bolstered by Gregory and O'Callaghan and this time they were

Ordinary Boys

Above: Highly-influential coach Oscar Arce.

Right: Lions Phil Walker and Dave Mehmet receive player and young player awards from George Petchey

Above: After Oscar - the Millwall youth team line-up with new coach David Payne (back row, far right) and minus Dave Mehmet who was on first team duty when the picture was taken.

Below: The doomed Super Den project is revealed.

99

Ordinary Boys

Ordinary Boys

Above and below: Heading for glory - Phil Coleman heads home the decisive second goal to give Millwall an unassailable lead over Manchester City.

Left top, Manchester City goalkeeper Alex Williams under pressure, watched by a packed Halfway Line, the official attendance was announced as just under 6,000. The actual figure is probably at least twice that.

Left, middle and bottom: Tony Kinsella on the attack.

Ordinary Boys

Above: Skipper Paul Roberts lifts the trophy and (below) celebrates with teammates.

Ordinary Boys

Above and below: The lap of honour

Ordinary Boys

Above: Coach David Payne can't hide his delight at the final whistle as he celebrates with captain Paul Roberts and striker Chris Dibble.

Below: Payne poses post-match proudly holding the trophy, flanked by Dave Mehmet and Phil Coleman

Ordinary Boys

Above - Smiles all round: Players, manager, directors and chairman toast their success. The team's reward would be a trip to Paris and an eventful tournament, culminating in a trip to the famous Moulin Rouge.

Below - One big happy family: Dean Horrix, Alan McKenna, Phil Coleman, David Payne, John Helps and Andy Massey.

Ordinary Boys

Above: Millwall Youth Team 1979-80 team photo, FA Youth Cup proudly on show, but with David Payne replaced by new coach Roger Cross.
Below: Chris Dibble in first team action at The Den

joined by youth skipper Roberts - just one month after his 17th birthday.

Many members of that victorious team were eligible to attempt to emulate Palace's feat of back-to-back wins the next season, but with the club facing yet more crippling financial woes and the prospect of Third Division football again, they were likely to be stepped up full time to first team duty for the 1979-80 campaign.

Not for the first time, Millwall football club's future was shrouded in uncertainty.

There was still of course one unfinished matter to be sorted: the bonus for winning the FA Youth Cup!

Herbert Burnige was true to his word and the team were indeed rewarded, as Phil Coleman remembers:

"As a reward for winning the final the chairman organised a trip to Paris for the whole squad."

"This consisted of four days in Paris, two days playing in a tournament and two days sightseeing. I told the lads I could speak French so I had offers from many to room with me, I could barely order a drink in French but rooming with Cally was a good laugh.

"The night before the tournament we played a Yugoslavian team in a keep ball session in the car park of the hotel. In 30 minutes we never got a kick, never got near them as they dominated us. When it came to a full game the next day we smashed them

9-0. We went on to win the tournament but not before the locals took offence to some of our 'traditional' Millwall tackles and aggression on their striker.

"Basically myself and Robbo battered him, culminating in us being locked in the changing rooms until a police escort was arranged to get us out of the stadium with the police telling us all to 'grab a bottle or studded boots to protect yourself'.

"Two days sightseeing in Paris meant a trip up the Eiffel Tower, brilliant views. The highlight being the fact that full back Tony Dark told us he was scared of heights so a few of us dragged him all the way to the very top, cannot think why he was shaking and looking rather pale!

"In the evening we had a paid trip to the famous Moulin Rouge. A bit of topless cancan dancing meant a few of the lads eyes were popping out their heads.

The bottle of free champagne on each table went down well but at 7 Francs for a bottle of beer we left sober but with some great memories."

Striker Alan McKenna also remembers the trip well:

"We couldn't believe we were going to the famous Moulin Rouge, and when we arrived we were pleased to discover the doorman was English. Even more so when he warned us how expensive the drinks were and advised us to pop to the bar next door for a few cheap lagers first!"

10

Look at What You Could Have Won

The story a few miles down the road at Crystal Palace was strikingly similar to Millwall's, but they were a few seasons ahead of their south London rivals and with a few vital differences.

By the time charismatic manager Malcolm Allison had decided that the future of the club's success lay in developing young, local talent, he had presided over a crushing double relegation from the top flight in 1973 to the Third Division. He quickly set about completely revamping the very foundations of the club and its impact was immediate.

As at Millwall, in-demand, talented young players favoured signing for them as word quickly spread that, if you proved your ability, there was a very good chance you would quickly get your chance in the first team.

Like Jago and Arce at The Den, Allison's training methods were way ahead of his time. The youngsters were cosseted like no others. He even put a stop to the age-old tradition of young apprentices doing the menial chores of cleaning boots of their senior pros and sweeping the terraces. Something that didn't always go down well with the older players at the club.

The main difference between the revolution that was beginning at Selhurst Park in 1974 and the similar one that would start at The Den a couple of years later was investment. Palace had already invested an obscene amount in obtaining the services of Allison and, even in their Third Division days, regularly attracted the sort of attendances that allowed for that investment to be continued.

The culture at Palace was also very different to that of Millwall. Gordon Jago tried unsuccessfully to push through a radical re-branding of the club which included renaming Cold Blow Lane Montego Bay Boulevard - or something similarly ill-becoming of the locale - and to make it more user-friendly and appealing to families and in turn attract higher gates to similarly reinvest in the club.

Fans quite rightly weren't having this. There is arguably a similar trade-off going on today when clubs so obviously sell their soul for success and Millwall continue to resist.

It easy to understand why and the fact that it is at the expense of success is far from proven – even to this day. All the rebranding in the world won't change the media perception of the club – and if anything will make them only more eager to drag the past up and throw it in their newly-branded faces again.

When Malcolm Allison left with his work just begun, he was succeeded by Terry Venables and progress was steady behind the scenes at Palace. Second Division status was regained after three seasons and by then they had secured the first of their back-to-back FA Youth Cup wins.

The healthy financial state of the club meant that squad could be kept together at that level as they were still eligible and a second successful season together while the first team continued to progress and the transition from a youth side that beat virtually everyone in its path to a first team capable of winning the Second Division championship within a couple of seasons was relatively smooth.

For Jago, Arce and Petchey at Millwall, there was Allison, John Cartwright and Terry Venables at Palace. Venables was a relative unknown at the time but, like Petchey, a coaching visionary. Cartwright was, like Arce, the likeable link for the youth players to the first team and always had Venables' ear.

When Palace gained promotion under Venables from the Third Division in 1977 and started life back in Division Two with a trip to The Den, two of their FA Youth Cup wining squad from the previous season made it into the starting line-up that day: Kenny Sansom and Vince Hilaire. Sansom was, like Mehmet in the Millwall side, a very young starter and already a regular in the team, Hilaire was making his debut and scored in the 3-0 win for Venables' men.

By the time the fixture was repeated at the start of the following season, most of that Palace youth team which had remained together and won it for a second time had made the successful transition into a first team comfortably holding its own in Division Two.

Sansom and Hilaire were joined by Gilbert, Nicholas, Murphy and Swindlehurst to repeat the 3-0 win and their upward trajectory continued to the top flight at the end of the season.

It was this environment that was so beneficial in Palace's grand plan of converting their youth success into first team triumph. There was absolutely no pressure on Venables whatsoever to use any of them in the first team who were coping easily with the rigours of life in Division Two thanks to the more experienced youth team graduates from three or four years earlier such as Jim Cannon, Nicky Chatterton and Paul Hinshelwood. They also had the benefit of experience of Ian Evans and George Graham - both future coaches in the making. Members of that Palace youth team talk about a very similar unity and feeling of invincibility that Millwall's veterans of 1979 recall.

Vince Hilaire was the lightning-quick, eye-catching winger that came through that side and remembers how they beat almost every side with ease that they faced – but Millwall was always a slightly tougher proposition:

"We were pretty much untouchable at Palace, but when we played Millwall we certainly knew we'd been in a game" He recalls.

"The thing is, a lot of the Palace lads and Millwall lads knew each other really well. A lot of us played either together or against each other in schools and county football."

Indeed a few of that Palace team that made it all the way to the First Division could have been part of Millwall's young revolution.

Camberwell-born Kenny Sansom and Milllwall-supporting Billy Gilbert were both on Bob Pearson's radar and even West Ham-supporting Hilaire who played a lot of his early football with Kevin O'Callaghan, Dave Martin and Paul Roberts could have ended up at The Den but proved to be the rare ones that got away for Pearson. In Arnie Warren, Palace had their very own Bob Pearson and between the two of them they probably unearthed some of the finest home-grown footballing talent of an entire generation for Palace, Millwall and later Queens Park Rangers.

Billy Gilbert had allegedly actually made it onto the hallowed Millwall turf at The Den prior to getting his big break at Palace. However it was as one of many Millwall supporters during the various stoppages for crowd disturbances during the FA Cup match against Ipswich!

Back at The Den, things were moving on again. Youth team coach David Payne barely had chance to bask in the glory of the FA Youth Cup win before he was off to pastures new.

He made the somewhat surprising and incongruous jump from Millwall to The Metropolitan Police. That is the football team, and not the constabulary.

Unfortunately for Payne, the move did not work out for him and he left the game.

He had spent exactly one year in his first - and as it turns out only - coaching job at a football league club and, even though it was only in a youth team capacity, had won the biggest competition it was possible to win.

The Crystal Palace/Orient formula for Millwall success had certainly worked its magic on the youngsters. Now Millwall desperately wanted it to work on the first team under former Palace and Os man George Petchey. Taking the reigns from Payne was another young coach - Roger Cross - who had the nucleus of that cup-winning side to work with, along with another handful of rising stars.

The challenge was now on to emulate Palace and win back to back titles, but would the demands of Petchey's first team and the increasing interest from the league's top clubs deprive Millwall of that feat?

Ordinary Boys

11

From Cleaning Kitch's Boots to the UEFA Cup

Millwall were always keen to bring in experienced staff to help at every level of the club and in the summer of 1979 they pulled off something of a coup.

Legendary coach Arthur Rowe arrived as a club consultant and took up an office with Bob Pearson. Rowe's playing career had started at Spurs but it was when he moved into coaching and management that he really made his mark after taking a 10 week coaching course in Hungary. War prevented him from taking up a three year contract offer there so he went on to become an Army PT and, alongside Matt Busby, took an army team on a tour of the rest camps in Italy and Greece. Once hostilities were over he was keen to progress back in England.

After cutting his managerial teeth at Chelmsford City just after the war and quickly turning them into a major non-league force, he took over at Second

Division Spurs in 1949 with the task of getting them back into the top flight.

Thanks to his brand of revolutionary 'push and run' football, it was a task that he not only fulfilled immediately, but he followed it up the following season with the First Division title.

Ill-health prevented him from growing his Tottenham legacy which led to a forced absence from the game but this gave him time to help develop and market the first lightweight football boot.

Once back to full health he returned to management taking Crystal Palace up from the Fourth Division and then settled at Orient in an advisory capacity to George Petchey. It was no doubt his friendship with Petchey that led to this influential figure in the game and his brief, part-time stay at The Den didn't go unnoticed – especially by Chris Dibble:

"I can remember going into the little stand at the old Den, where the gym was, up the little stairs and there was Arthur and he used to say: 'look mate, just remember the give-and-go movement, that's what made Tottenham, and it'll make you' and he was right, we played a pass and move style and it worked".

"He was such a nice man to talk to. When you had a problem Bob Pearson would say: 'go and have a word with Arthur.' I loved to talk about the game and I'll always remember chatting to him."

Petchey it seemed was doing everything in his power to wrap his young charges in the cotton wool of footballing experience.

There were two inherent threats to Millwall's still-blossoming young stars as the club started life back in the Third Division. The first was the uncompromising playing style that was par for the course at that level. Division Three 70s and 80s style was direct, unforgiving and certainly not a stage for the steady development of skills in the way that Oscar Arce had taught. This was a world away from that. Forget tika taka, this was traditional kick, bollock and bite.

Secondly, the danger of so many of that successful youth team playing - and now starring - regularly for the first team was that they were now very much on the radar of bigger clubs and seen as easy pickings toiling away at a struggling Third Division side.

One such example was Kevin O'Callaghan. The skilful winger was now one of the first names on George Petchey's team sheet and scored five goals in the first six matches of the new season.

Roberts and Mehmet were also first team regulars by now, playing in the first 12 games, and when Roberts was rested, his place was taken by fellow youth cup winner Gregory. In fairness to Petchey, he was well-versed in the correct way to blood young players and wasn't just chucking them in at the deep end without help. They were joined in the team by seasoned professionals such as John Jackson in goal, Mel Blyth and Dave Donaldson.

In fact it was a blend that seemed to be working a treat when, following a shaky start, after those first twelve matches the team entertained Sheffield Wednesday at The Den in a pulsating 3-3 draw as the division's top side.

By now however injury had robbed the side of O'Callaghan who returned at the end of the year with the team now down to seventh place. He played three more matches, before it was announced that a £250,000 fee had been agreed with Bobby Robson's Ipswich Town. It was a record transfer for a 17-year-old at the time and an offer far too good for either party to turn down.

O'Callaghan's arrival at Millwall had been typical of the path that most of the class of '79 had taken, when a host of clubs were sniffing around the footballing talent at the time:

"I was doing the rounds, going on trial at different clubs and then Bob Pearson came on the scene and wanted me to go to Millwall. There was something there that told me it was going places. I could have signed for anyone at the time but I chose Millwall, I knew I'd have more chance of getting in the first team there and that was one of the main reasons really."

The genuine opportunity of a place in the first team if you were good enough, rather than old enough, was an incentive that was only being offered at one other club: Crystal Palace - and that was what enabled both Millwall and Palace to have first refusal on much of the London young footballing talent at the time.

One of his first memories was being part of the team that almost knocked Crystal Palace's team of young invincibles off their perch and as an apprentice, being assigned to one of Millwall's all-time greats.

"I remember in my first season we played Crystal Palace in the Southern Junior Floodlit Cup. They were beating everyone at the time and although we lost we really gave them a game. We were pretty much all schoolboys at the time and the next season we were just different class."

"The team spirit was amazing, Barry Kitchener once told me I was the worst apprentice he'd ever had because I didn't clean his boots properly, but he was great, he just laughed about it, he used to lend me his car. I wasn't interested in cleaning boots, I just wanted to play football"

Kevin also has fond memories of his first coach and sad ones of his sudden exit:

"I loved Oscar, he was brilliant, he liked working with skilful players. We came in one day and he just disappeared. He was training one day and then he just didn't come in and I never spoke to him again, it was a shame."

When the time came to leave The Den, it was almost as sudden.

"There was a lot of speculation around about America but I didn't want to go there. At the time, the banks had foreclosed on the club, Ipswich came in with an offer of £250,000, I spoke to Bobby Robson and that was it."

Robson's Ipswich - who had battered Millwall 6-1 in that ill-fated FA Cup quarter final just two years before on their way to winning the trophy were genuine contenders for the Division One title and European honours and the next season, with O'Callaghan in the team, they reached the semi-finals of the FA Cup, achieved a runners-up place in the First Division and glory in Europe.

In the blink of an eye, Kevin O'Callaghan had gone from cleaning Barry Kitchener's boots to the UEFA Cup final.

His final match for Millwall was a crushing 4-0 defeat away to Carlisle and whilst his departure was not solely responsible for the club's fall from promotion contention, it was very much the beginning of the end. O'Callaghan would go on to help write probably the most significant chapter in Millwall's history - and play a part in another - but not for some time, as The Lions nosedive continued.

The American interest was bizarre - and would return. Football (soccer) was being heavily pushed in the states again - and it was where ex-Millwall boss Gordon Jago was now realising his coaching vision.

Then, as today with the MLS, there was a clamber to sign aging ex-professional household names of the game which lured the likes of Pele, Best and Marsh, but they were also keen to snare young talent too - no doubt at the behest of Jago.

Whilst it was never confirmed in writing, Millwall had, earlier that season, apparently received an incredible £1 million joint bid for O'Callaghan, Mehmet and Tony Kinsella - arguably the three most technically gifted members of the club. The offer fizzled out as Millwall were at the time top of the league and looking to fend off any interest in their star players as they looked to make a swift return to the second tier.

Petchey's patched-up Lions won just five out of 23 matches after O'Callaghan left but his departure was so much more than just an impact on results, it was a watershed.

The whole point of the inception of the youth system at Millwall was that, with transfer fees and wages slowly starting to creep up, the 1970s saw the first real gap begin to open up between the top teams.

With the game in what seemed like an ever-spiralling decline as hooliganism and recession affected crowds, clubs like Millwall quickly found themselves living beyond their means.

Once they had sold off the assets that they had managed to unearth from the lower leagues, there was no-where else to turn, which is why the youth system was so vital. This conveyor of young talent, whilst it wouldn't always be as productive as the class of '79, should have been Millwall's insurance policy. It should have made them future-proof, now it too it seemed was being sold off.

Millwall fans had seen it all before. Just when they felt they were on the verge of building a team capable of achieving that all-elusive top flight place, the key player would be sold on to keep the wolf from the door. Hurley, Possee, King, Hill.

Now they thought there was finally a chance and that luck was on their side, as soon as they had invested serious time and money in a youth system it was bearing fruit, yet once again it was simply being sold off to pay the bills, leaving the club deeper than ever in the mire.

12

Throwing it All Away

As with the previous season, it was the youths that provided relief from the doom and gloom at first team level.

The latest crop of youngsters looked to be ready to emulate Palace's back-to-back triumphs after beating Reading, Ipswich, Southampton and Middlesbrough, on their way to the last four but came up against an Aston Villa side that managed what so many other teams couldn't - to win at The Den - and the midlands side's 2-0 first leg victory in Millwall's own back yard proved enough to wrestle the trophy from The Lions' grasp.

Villa were, at the time, on their way to winning the League title and European Cup, another measure of how Millwall's humble youth team was able to push the very biggest and best of oppositions at that time.

It was a side that retained two from the previous season's winning squad - Tony Kinsella and Andy

Massey - along with two names that would eventually graduate to become regulars at first team level in Keith Stevens and Paul Sansome. There's little doubt that if those players that were now regulars in the first team but still eligible to be picked for the competition had played, Millwall would have indeed matched those back-to-back wins that Palace achieved.

But as Dave Mehmet remembers, football was now very different for the skilful young stars of that final triumph:

"I remember playing a league match away one midweek night at Chesterfield I think it was. They were all six footers and I looked around and we had nine youth team players plus John Jackson and Barry Kitchener. They just battered us. Physically we weren't strong enough, nothing to do with football and a few of the boys, deep down, found it too much and that's why a lot of them went out of the game altogether."

As a new season began, The Den's exit door remained busy with three of the first team's more senior and influential members sold off. John Seasman and Tony Towner left for Rotherham for a combined total of £185,000 and John Lyons left for Cambridge for £100,000.

This meant that in the space of just over six months, Millwall had basically stripped itself of its most talented assets: the creative flair of O'Callaghan,

Seasman and Towner, and the all-important goals of Lyons in return for what appeared to be the princely sum of over half a million pounds.

It's a figure that a few third tier clubs would be grateful for today and could probably use to make a marked improvement in their first team's fortunes. For Millwall through, it appeared to simply disappear into a bottomless pit of debt.

A fact that was borne out by just how much of it they eventually managed to invest: £6,000.

That was the fee for non-league goalscoring sensation John Bartley who arrived from Athenian League Welling United having scored 70 goals in each of his last three seasons.

It was to prove yet another example of right player, wrong time though. As with the emerging youth team talent, introducing a player untested at that level in a struggling side was always doomed to failure and even though Bartley did well considering the woeful state of affairs around him at the club at the time, it was far too little, too late.

With no disrespect to Bartley, it was a gesture that smacked of a hardened gambler throwing his last few quid on a rank outsider in the hope that by some outrageous turn of fortune it would come in and all would be OK again.

Everywhere Millwall fans turned they were being haunted by the players their club had allowed to leave.

Match of The Day viewers saw O'Callaghan scoring his first goal for Ipswich - a strike which was also nominated as Goal of the Month - and as the 1980-81 season descended into a gloomy November with The Lions already in the Third Division relegation places, top of the table Rotherham romped to a 3-0 victory with both Towner and Seasman running the show.

It was a third consecutive defeat for a team that incredibly now included seven of the youth cup winning side in the twelve-man squad. It could have been more with Gleasure, Gregory, Mehmet and Massey also featuring during those bleak opening 18 league matches.

To the outsider, it was a case of the class of '79 simply not being up to it, but it was fairly obvious to anyone who knew the game that the protective foil that any young player needs in first team football - that of experienced pros playing around them for the gruelling 90 minutes of being kicked and shoved that was Division Three in 1980 - had been quickly eroded and they were being hung out to dry.

Reinforcements arrived in the shape of defender John Sitton who himself was a recent graduate of the Chelsea youth system - and although slightly older, still didn't have the necessary experience to carry the rest of them through.

Following that Rotherham defeat, manager Petchey ordered the team back for extra training on Sunday morning. It's a gesture that older pros are well familiar with.

Not so much a punishment for the players - although as you can imagine, few are impressed at having to sacrifice their Sunday rest - but more a show of intent to the board that he intends to take immediate steps to rectify the situation.

For Petchey though, it was too late and he was relieved of his first team duties on the eve of the next home match. It seemed harsh on Petchey who, from day one in his Millwall managerial career, had been fighting fires from several directions.

The fallout from Panorama, the club's worsening financial plight and the task of gently blooding a crop of youth players that were essential for the future of the club were all plates that Petchey had been successfully spinning for three years but it was inevitable that it would all come crashing down around him eventually.

Initially, recognising that Petchey was still an extremely talented coach and the value of keeping him at the club with his knowledge of the set-up, rather than being shown the door he was moved upstairs with the title of 'General Manager'. A 1980 version of 'Director of Football I suppose you could say but, as in the current era where few actually know what a Director of Football's true function is, it was a nothing position that itself would soon come to just that and Petchey eventually left for Brighton.

As 1980 drew to a close, America came knocking on Millwall's door once more, only this time it was to give rather than attempt to take and it had a very strong Millwall connection.

Gordon Jago was coach at Tampa Bay Rowdies, the glamorous, sun-kissed Florida club couldn't have been more removed from the crumbling, grey depressed Den in December 1980 and they were reaching out an arm of help across the pond in the shape of a new, young, player-manager for Millwall.

Peter Anderson had enjoyed a reasonably successful career at Luton before joining Jago in Florida. He was now looking for his first coaching assignment and where better than at Millwall?

At 31, Anderson arrived as Millwall's player-manager in what looked like a win-win situation for all concerned.

Here was a young manager who could also bring much-needed experience to the playing side and, having played under Gordon Jago, the man who had began the young revolution at Millwall, he would surely be the perfect man to resurrect the club's fortunes and get the most out of their talented youth. All looked well at the start and within a month of taking over he had guided The Lions to 16th spot and relative safety with a win at Chester. Anderson played himself in a side that included Martin, Roberts, Kinsella, Massey, Mehmet and Horrix. In fact it was Anderson who scored the only goal of the game to earn the win at a ground that had rarely been a productive one for Millwall - even given the club's famously poor away record - and in 1980-81 it was particularly poor. When Anderson took over the side had just a single point from a 1-1 draw at Fulham to show from 11 away trips.

On Boxing Day they travelled to Gillingham for Anderson's first away match in charge. Such were the celebrations that greeted Alan McKenna's 83rd minute winner from both player and fans that the young Scottish striker (who was starting to reproduce some of his youth team goalscoring form in the first team) received a visit from the local constabulary after the match.

"I was getting changed after the match and we were all celebrating the win when there was a knock on the door and a policeman appeared." Recalls McKenna.

"He basically told me that my goal celebrations were over the top and could have caused crowd trouble!"

It was true that Millwall's away form was criminal, but that was surely taking it too far.

The club remained in the bottom half of the table for the rest of the season but were rarely looking over their shoulder at the relegation places and Anderson continued to place faith in the young pros with Dibble and Gleasure also featuring.

Anderson had also made some moves in the transfer market to plug the gaps left by the fire sale of the previous 18 months and winger Austin Hayes arrived to provide some much-needed craft and experience.

Bartley was finding the net and seemed to be striking up a decent front line partnership with Horrix and even Lions legend Barry Kitchener made a welcome return to the first team after suffering a broken ankle.

Finally the team appeared to have a balance of youth and experience, all they needed now was some financial stability for the club as a whole. Then came another bombshell.

Completely out of the blue, both Dave Mehmet and Tony Kinsella were sold to Tampa Bay Rowdies. With rumours of offers in excess of £1 million being tabled by First Division clubs and rebuffed by The Lions' board, the unconfirmed reports that the talent two had been whisked across the Atlantic to join Jago for little more than £200,000 understandably infuriated fans, compelling the club to offer an explanation boldly entitled: "TONY KINSELLA AND DAVID MEHMET - THE REASONS WHY" in the opening pages of its matchday programme for the home game with Barnsley on 20th March 1981:

"We have been inundated with complaints from fans for not only selling these two players but letting

them go at giveaway prices. There was no way we wanted Tony and David to leave but, quite simply, if the deal hadn't gone through we would have gone out of business. Millwall, like many other clubs in the Football League, is losing money. Our average gates of 4,300 mean that we have a revenue loss of between £4,000 and £5,000 each week amounting to some £550,000 for the last two seasons. With such heavy losses we can only keep our head above water for so long before we have to sell players to relieve the financial pressure. But also remember that we have bought players as well for some £583,000. We have been criticised for accepting such a low fee for these players. Naturally we would have liked more but this was the only offer we received and the days of the £1 million plus transfer fees are over, at least for the time being. There is also no truth in the original £1 million offer from Tampa Bay last season which was denied by the club itself, or the suggestions in the press that a number of our players are wanted by such and such a club. We are doing everything in our power to reduce losses by cutting expenditure and raising revenue off the field through the Lions Lottery. Thanks to your efforts

Sales of tickets have increased considerably in recent weeks since Peter Anderson made his appeal for 1,000 agents, while additional income has been received from supporters renewing their season tickets for next season. As we go to press an announcement is expected to be made within the next 7 days which will greatly strengthen our financial base as well as assuring the club's future. It will enable us to go forward from a position of strength. When you hear of the financial plight of former FA Cup winners such as Newcastle United, Derby County and Cardiff City, this statement will become even more significant. It can only be good news for Millwall and give Peter Anderson the financial muscle to strengthen the team. You too can play your part in helping the Millwall renaissance. We still need many more Lottery agents and details of how to apply are contained in the programme. Alternatively, why not call into the club or the commercial office after today's match? Millwall is your club. We know that most of the news coming out of the Den in the past has disappointed us all but the tide is turning with better days ahead with the club now in a position to fulfil its true potential.

UP THE LIONS!"

That final "UP THE LIONS" must have felt like a very hollow clarion call to the fans who could now only pray that their beloved club didn't slip further into oblivion.

Those prayers then, equally out of the blue, appeared to be answered.

Millionaire businessman Alan Thorne - a relative of Tom Thorne who had presided over the club's move across the river to The Den in 1910 - took over from the beleaguered Len Eppel and his first words to Millwall's long-suffering fans must have been music to their ears:

"The first promise I want to make to the supporters of Millwall FC as chairman is that no players will be sold purely for financial reasons. The only players that will be leaving this club are the ones that your manager feels must go for football reasons only. This policy is essential if my dreams as a lifelong Lions supporter are to be realised and Millwall are to become a First Division club."

Thorne took on the club's estimated £750,000 debts, and with the promise of investment in the team instead of asset-stripping, this would surely mean that finally the hard work that had gone into producing a young, talented, home-grown Millwall team could finally be seen to fruition.

Outgoing incumbent Leonard Eppel's time at the club had seen some of the leanest times in the club's history and his elaborate plans to develop the stadium (which were now seemingly in tatters) had met with similar mocking to Noah building his ark.

Eppel however would go on to prove that his big ideas had substance. Something of a visionary, he turned his attention north and set about the regeneration of Liverpool's Albert Dock. Once again, those who he unveiled his plans to thought it was the work of fantasy but, unperturbed, he set about the project with his London-based development company Arrowcroft in partnership with the Merseyside Development Corporation to restore the former industrial stronghold.

Eppel almost single-handedly convinced his board that the unique atmosphere of the dock should not be lost.

He considered the restoration to be his greatest achievement, for which he was awarded a CBE.

The life-long Millwall fan was even made an "Honorary Scouser" by the Lord Mayor of Liverpool Steve Rotheram in 2009.

Paying tribute to Eppel following his death in 2012 at the age of 84, Mayor of Liverpool Joe Anderson paid tribute to Mr Eppel, saying he was "a key player in the renaissance of the city."

It was some tribute to a man whose brief spell at the club he loved was so punctuated with unfulfilled promise. It was also clearly Millwall's loss, because what transpired next was more revolt than revolution.

13

And Then There Was One

Anderson had arrived from Florida and seemed to have a positive influence on the club as a whole, also appearing to embrace the policy of putting faith in youth. But when news broke that both Dave Mehmet and Tony Kinsella were off to join Jago at Tampa Bay, questions were being asked on The Den terraces as fans gathered to watch their team start a new season with two more talents from the class of '79 absent.

Little information was made public about any transfer fee received by the club for the pair. Whether it came close pro-rata to the £1 million that had supposedly been bid for Mehmet, Kinsella and O'Callaghan two years before is unlikely and closer to the truth is the unconfirmed aforementioned £200,000.

Conspiracy theorists might have suspected that the deal was in fact a straight swap for Anderson with the full transaction intended to be made in the summer of 1981 but with the Anderson move expedited in an attempt to help Millwall stay up and solve their managerial vacancy. We'll never know.

Like many of his colleagues, the story Tony Kinsella was given by Anderson when he broke the news of his imminent departure was that the decision was a financial one:

"It was heart breaking when I had to leave the club because I really loved it there but Anderson explained to me and Dave Mehmet that the club was skint and we had to go." Kinsella remembers.

"We were travelling back from an away game on the coach and Anderson called me down to the front and explained they'd had an offer from Tampa Bay Rowdies and that I needed to go along to a hotel in London the following night with my mum and dad to meet Gordon Jago."

The deal was done shortly after, despite interest from First Division Everton who were ready to table a reported bid of £175,000, both Kinsella and Mehmet crossed the Atlantic for an undisclosed fee thought to be little more than the Merseysiders' opening gambit for Kinsella alone.

Kinsella was remarkably undaunted signing a four year contract to play in the USA as an eighteen year old:

"It was phenomenal because at that time I didn't know much about the game in America, I didn't even know what the standard was like, but Gordon Jago told us that we had Frank Worthington and John Gorman joining us along with Kevin Keelan, David Moss and the rest of the team was made up of former full internationals from different countries."

With hindsight though, Kinsella agrees that the move was probably the wrong one at the wrong time and he would have been better with a move to a top English club as Kevin O'Callaghan did with Ipswich.

As Mehmet recalls, he too was given little choice about the move:

"Gordon Jago offered £200,000 for me and Tony Kinsella. I was told we needed the money. I didn't want to go, I said no and this went on for about six weeks. In the end Millwall paid me to leave, that's what it had come to."

Another aspect of Anderson's stewardship that hadn't gone unnoticed was the fact that he had seemingly lost faith in no less than four central defenders at the club.

Youth players Phil Coleman and Paul Robinson who had already successfully made the step up to Petchey's sides, John Sitton who had slotted in well since his arrival from Chelsea and the club's legendary stalwart Barry Kitchener were nowhere to be seen.

Whilst Kitchener was now approaching 35, he still had the vital experience both in terms of playing and of over a decade of being at the club to contribute and should have been an obvious choice to join Anderson in a coaching capacity while retaining his player registration.

It was highly likely however that Anderson perhaps saw him as a threat, but the omission of Coleman, Robinson and Sitton remained a mystery.

That aside, a starting line-up that contained Gleasure, Roberts, Martin, Dibble, Horrix and Massey alongside the experience of Phil Warman, Nicky Chatterton and the second of Anderson's recruits - ex-Luton teammate Alan West was good enough to start the season with a win over Preston at The Den.

Defeat was tasted just twice in the first two months of the season and by the time it came, another new signing was in the team. Sam Allardyce had arrived from Sunderland for £90,000 - a considerable chunk of change for Millwall and for a 29-year-old centre back - especially when it wasn't exactly a position Millwall were lacking in.

Allardyce's top-flight experience was certainly taking some time to rub off on the Millwall defence though as, in his fifth match for the club they slipped to defeat by the odd goal in nine in a bizarre match at Exeter. The 5-4 reverse wasn't as close as the final score suggests with The Lions 0-3 down within

25 minutes and trailing 1-5 with well over twenty minutes left.

A late flurry of goals gave the scoreline a somewhat distorted appearance - and Anderson the perfect excuse to begin his destruction of Millwall.

One of the first out of the door was Alan McKenna. Less than twelve months after netting the winner in that away win at Gillingham, he was transferred north of the border to Berwick Rangers. His ten months playing under Anderson was typically bizarre and it was made fairly clear once he didn't figure in the manager's plans as he remembers:

"Peter Anderson was great at first, I think it was the same for a lot of the players. Then, one day, he just suddenly stopped talking to you!"

Phil Coleman was transferred to Colchester for the ridiculously cheap fee of £15,000. Coleman did not want to leave - a decision that he felt even more passionate about after visiting Essex for talks with the recently-relegated Fourth Division side.

His arm was twisted however when it was made clear to him by Anderson that he did not figure in his first team plans - and also by a director who hinted that, despite new chairman Thorne's promises, the wolves were once again at the door and the £15,000 was needed to meet that month's wage bill.

If Coleman left his beloved Lions with the distinct impression that he had not been fed the truth, he was to be proved entirely correct. Just over a year before the club had apparently turned down a reported £400,000 bid from Brighton manager Alan Mullery when they were in arguably a far more parlous financial state. Sitton too was on his way - a move to Gillingham rushed through with similar finesse to the Coleman transfer. Something wasn't right.

Life certainly wasn't dull at The Den under Peter Anderson during the 1981/82 season - the first in which the new three points for a win system was introduced, meaning a quick run of defeats could see you toppled from a promotion place - as Millwall discovered at the start of the season - and similarly, stringing three or four wins together could see you back in contention.

That wasn't quite how it worked out for Millwall but as things settled down and a lower mid-table position became a respectable final finish of ninth, it was enough to give fans, manager and, more importantly as the man with the cheque book - chairman Thorne, cause for optimism for the next season.

The dreadfully drab and toothless football that had been produced prior to Anderson's arrival had been replaced by, at times, bright, exciting and expansive play, but was worryingly lacking in discipline.

A point outlined by the nine-goal madness at Exeter which was avenged by thumping the Devon side 5-1 at The Den later in the season; 4-3 home victories over eventual champions Burnley and runners-up Fulham;

thrilling 3-2 and 3-3 league cup clashes with Orient and Oxford, then heavy defeats at mid-table Brentford (1-4) and Reading (0-4) and eventually relegated Bristol City (1-4). Even the FA Cup produced goals with Portsmouth being ousted 3-2 in a replay only for Grimsby to hit the Lions for six on a shocking third round night at The Den.

On the surface, Anderson was continuing to keep faith with youth. He gave first team debuts to goalkeeper Paul Sansome - who was now vying with FA Youth Cup winner Gleasure for the number one jersey - and full back Keith Stevens. By the end of the season there also seemed to be hope for Paul Robinson who played in the final five matches.

What was probably not quite right was the blend of experience. The likes of Lawrie Madden, Graham Paddon, Bobby Shinton, and Alan Slough, along with Hayes and West made just cameo appearances instead of forming a consistent foil for the younger players.

Allardyce had proved to be a consistent performer with 41 appearances throughout the season - but as some of those scorelines suggest, the defence as a unit was anything but consistent.

One highlight was the arrival of Dean Neal. A young striker who had arrived from QPR and weighed in with five goals from his twenty appearances. Here, Millwall fans felt, was a player who would truly compliment the team and the young players. In the summer of 1982, Millwall embarked on unprecedented team-building investment - both in terms of transfer fees and wages paid for two new players. One of the new recruits had excited Lions fans raising a glass - but others had them raising an eyebrow.

The first looked to be a perfect fit for Millwall. Trevor Aylott was a Bermondsey boy but had come through the ranks at Chelsea. After failing to make it at Stamford Bridge, he moved to Barnsley where 26 goals in 96 appearances helped the Yorkshire club win promotion as Third Division runners-up two seasons before and cement their place in Division Two.

At six feet tall and with a proven goalscoring record in the division above, his capture seemed something of a coup and would provide much-needed power in The Lions' front line.

The second recruit was 32-year-old midfielder Willie Carr from Wolves,

These days there are plenty of players performing at the highest level well in excess of that age, but things were very different back in 1982 when even the signing of Allardyce at 29 was considered risky with many players hanging up their boots soon after their 30th.

It was true that Millwall were in desperate need of some guile and experience in the middle of the park along with some guidance for the younger players, but alarm bells were ringing for Paul Robinson the first time he met Carr at training:

"We'd plucked Willie Carr out of Wolves reserves and he said to me 'I don't know what I'm doing here, both my knees are fucked, but they've offered me fantastic money to come and play' but he was knackered. Lovely man Willie, great fella, but that's what Anderson did. He brought in players he'd played with in the past or that he knew." Robinson recalls.

Millwall supporters were of course not privy to such revelations and will have been hoping that Carr could maintain his fitness as some other pros who were able to continue into their thirties had done - although they were very much the exception to the rule.

Hidden away amongst the furore of those two new arrivals was the departure of another of Millwall's FA Youth Cup winning side. Chris Dibble had hardly put a foot wrong, giving literally everything each time he pulled on the shirt and weighing in with five goals in 65 appearances. He was released to join Fourth Division Wimbledon.

The usual hum-drum of pre-season friendlies was bolstered by a new competition. The Football League Trophy was created to provide the lower divisions' teams (and a couple from the lower half of Division Two) with an opportunity to win some silverware.

It began with a four-team group competition and gave Millwall fans the perfect opportunity to see their new recruits in competitive action before the league programme kicked off up at Preston. For added spice, as it was regionalised for the early group stage, it pitted them against fellow London sides Wimbledon, Brentford and Crystal Palace.

Aylott and Carr made their official Millwall bows in a less-than-satisfactory 0-1 defeat at home to Fourth Division Wimbledon in the first match but there was plenty to suggest that the new faces were settling when Aylott scored in the next match - a 3-0 victory over Brentford. Also encouraging was that Dean Neal was also on the scoresheet and a Neal/Aylott strike-force appeared to bode well.

Millwall travelled to Crystal Palace for the first competitive game between the two sides since 1979 when The Eagles were on their way to claiming the Second Division championship and the title of 'Team of the Eighties' with their own FA Youth Cup-inspired side.

The Millwall fans that made the short trip across south London were delighted to see their side secure a second 3-0 win with two more goals from Neal and one from Palace old boy Chatterton. They would have been equally impressed to see Willie Carr start his third game in a week, being subbed for Shinton after featuring for the full ninety minutes in the first two ties.

Neal and Chatterton were on the scoresheet again a week later when Anderson took his side to Preston for their first league match of the new season. Unfortunately, by the time Chatterton had scored his side's first in the 54th minute, his side were already 0-2 down and on their way to a 2-3 opening day defeat in what looked like a very similar story to the previous season.

Undeterred, the club put on a positive front for the first home league game at The Den and fans reading the programme will have been treated to an onslaught of good vibes from both manager and chairman.

In his notes for the match against Cardiff, Anderson hailed the arrival of Aylott and Carr and hinted at the change in mood towards the young squad members and Chris Dibble departure:

"They say that actions speak louder than words and I hope by now that every Millwall supporter has noted the arrival of our two new boys Willie Carr and Trevor Aylott.

Their appearance in the Lions team at the start of the new season spells out to everyone our intentions of competing with the best and challenging for honours this season.

Millwall fans have, in the past few years, become used to bidding farewell to their favourite players but thanks to Chairman Alan Thorne, we have succeeded in reversing that process.

While other clubs spent the close season fretting about their futures we went out with the positive attitude of strengthening our team and bringing a higher standard of football to the Den.

We were incredibly fortunate to get a player of the proven quality and experience of Scottish International Willie. Carr. He is a player I have long admired for his natural talents and his enthusiastic approach to the game.

He is a great passer of the ball who, even at 32, showed his tremendous appetite for the game when he won back his place in Wolves First Division side last season, discovering a new lease of life under the new management.

Willie is the sort of player I feel that I can look to not only to doing the stuff on the pitch but also in helping to guide our younger players. The arrival of Trevor Aylott, chased by a number of First Division clubs and one of the biggest transfer deals of the close season, is further proof of the chairman's determination not to accept second best.

I am convinced that Trevor is going to become one of the great heroes of Millwall. He is tailor made for the club. A Londoner through and through, this

Bermondsey boy is the sort of centre forward who cannot give any less than 100 per cent.

He is a player you, the fan, will be able to relate to and, to my mind, he is one of the best signings the club has ever made. He is an excellent player who we thoroughly scouted before convincing him that Millwall were a club he could make progress with and it showed a lot of courage on the part of the chairman to gamble on a player whose fee was an unknown quantity.

Not only did we clinch the signatures of these two top players but also we resisted the temptation of selling our top youngsters. The players we released we let go because, basically, we could not promise them first team football.

This especially applied to Dibble and Tagg who knew that, if they stayed, their opportunities would have been severely limited. Our aim is to improve and strengthen our squad at all times and despite our big outlay, we will continue to bring in the right players if we think they are needed.

It is imperative that we have not just a good team but a good squad -- and that is how I see my own role as a player. I have retained my registration and I will see how the season goes but as far as I am concerned

I am one more player who can help the club get what it wants promotion."

It wasn't revealed exactly which young stars the club had resisted offers for, but given the release of Mehmet and Kinsella and the treatment levelled at the likes of Coleman, Robinson and Dibble so far in Anderson's brief reign it was hard to understand who they could have been - or to believe his comments about new signing Carr helping the youngsters, as there weren't that many left!

Equally bullish was Chairman Alan Thorne who had allowed himself the centre spread of the programme to inform fans of a variety of club news from new catering arrangements to the sale of Lottery tickets. There were three very pertinent items though, all of which will have had Millwall fans in two minds as to how great this new revolution was going to be.

Firstly, he provided an update on the now long-protracted 'Super Den' project which had recently seemed to hit the buffers:

"Redevelopment of the Den

Although our plans looked like collapsing when Asda withdrew at the end of the last season just at the point when contracts were due to be signed, the scheme is still very much alive and kicking. The Lewisham Borough Council has given me complete charge of the project and we have now identified and ironed out the various problems, which partly caused the Asda deal to fall through. We have appointed Hillier Parker May & Rowden, an international firm of Chartered Surveyors with vast experience of shopping schemes, as our professional advisors. They have prepared a preliminary development brief setting out exactly what can be built at The Den. This has now been to all major supermarket chains and retailers for consideration and an invitation to enter into initial discussions. The next step will be to draw up a short list and, hopefully, before the end of this season we will be in a position to appoint our partners in this joint venture."

If Millwall fans had been sceptical about the idea when it was first revealed some four years before, they would really be doubting its credibility now. It appeared the project had progressed about as much as the team's fortunes and was becoming nothing more than an irritating distraction.

Next came something of a bombshell in terms of actually watching Millwall play right now - or at least in the near future. In a move some years ahead of its time, Thorne revealed that he was considering a fan identity card scheme:

"We are considering introducing identity cards at the earliest opportunity to encourage family support by making the Den absolutely safe for parents and children to come and watch football. Hooliganism and violence have been the unacceptable face of football for far too long and the main cause of falling gates

and must be stamped out if the game is to survive. We are currently finalising our plans but we envisage that supporters requiring an identity card will have to give us their name, address and two passport-size photos. The ground will be divided into two or three sections, the majority for card holders and the others for opposing fans and non-identity card-holders.

Fulham have said they hope to introduce the system fairly shortly and if the idea catches on with other clubs we may also have a section for their card-holders. If a fan misbehaves the card will be withdrawn and the only sections of the Den they could enter will be with opposing supporters where, hopefully, they will be in a minority or in non-card areas.

You will not be able to move from one part of the ground to another. If we find there is a minority group keeping a greater number of people away we may even close the part of the ground they use. We will also try and split up any other trouble making groups.

You may think we are trying to take away people's identity. In fact, we are trying to do completely the opposite and safeguard it by making the Den a place where you can come and watch football in complete safety and have an enjoyable day out with the whole family. We would very much like our supporters' views with respect to this scheme."

Thorne was extremely vocal in his opposition to football hooliganism, but as a fan himself, he must have appreciated the delicate nature in which it needed to be dealt with at Millwall.

His suggestion that any fan misbehaving would only be able to get in the ground in the away end was nothing short of outrageous and surely fanning the flames. If he felt hooliganism was having a detrimental effect on attendances, he would have been in for an almighty shock had he managed to progress beyond this staggering proposal as Lions fans would have stayed away in their thousands had they been expected to provide their name, address and passport photos to watch mid-table Third Division football!

The final one was a double-whammy with the news that - as fans that had already clicked through the turnstiles will have noticed - entrance prices had been increased. There was also a cautionary tale, wrapped up neatly in the news of Wolves recent salvation from going under, about the club's finances which they were led to believe were now secure under millionaire Thorne:

Reluctantly we have to increase the price of ground admission to £2.50 for Adults and £1.80 for O.A.Ps and Children under 16-years-of-age, with similar increases for Stand tickets £4.00 and £3.50. My current policy to admission prices is to try and hold them for a minimum of two seasons. Although gates last season were slightly up on the previous year we are still losing money to the tune of £4,000 per week.

The running of a football club is a precarious business and I dread to think what would have happened if Derek Dougan hadn't managed to save Wolves from going under three minutes from the receiver's deadline. Too many clubs are badly financed. The huge transfer fees are now largely historic apart from isolated cases mainly involving overseas clubs. If such an old and respected club as Wolves had gone the "knock-on" effect would have been catastrophic. It would certainly have panicked the banks after all it was Lloyds who pulled out the plug on Wolves and there is no doubt many clubs would have quickly gone to the wall. Millwall would certainly have survived but only because I personally guarantee our overdraft currently in excess of £1 million. However, no one person can continue indefinitely to finance the heavy losses we are incurring at the moment. Hopefully, the big investment we have made on new players will soon start coming through on the pitch with good results and increased gates. But we need an average attendance of 12,000 to even break even and there is no club in the Football League where attendances last season slumped by a record two million which can survive on its gate receipts alone."

This news being digested by any Millwall supporters that were reading it before the match kicked off was probably met with a mixture of trepidation and excitement that things seemed to be changing at the club, mostly for the better but there would certainly have been anger at the identity card proposals.

By the time the match had ended - with Cardiff romping to a 4-0 win - identity cards and new stadiums couldn't have been further from their thoughts.

By Christmas, Anderson was gone, Millwall were heading for the Fourth Division, and the class of '79 were all but disbanded, or cast aside in the reserves.

With the power of hindsight, Peter Anderson's stateside sabbatical was the death knell for his brief managerial career.

When you look right across what he tried to do at Millwall, it had a striking resemblance to the equally ill-fated US soccer project that he'd played under Gordon Jago at Tampa Bay Rowdies in.

The theory was great. A blend of youth and experience, the brightest stars of the future, combined with experienced pros - what could go wrong?

What went wrong was that, far from looking to put the icing on the cake of their illustrious careers and help develop the game in America, the aging pros that arrived in the US were simply there for one final pay day - and for most it was in the sun. Who could blame them?

They were being paid large amounts and they could go through the motions, there would be no outcry from the terraces that would have greeted them in England - or any of the other countries from across the globe where they had plied their trade previously.

Peter Anderson clearly felt he could do the same at Millwall. When he swapped the sun of Tampa for the gloom of south London, the project in America was still very much up and running, yet it capitulated almost simultaneously with his at The Den, doomed from the very start.

What was unforgiveable was the money made available to him by the new club owners to bring in aging pros who were neither fit enough or had the inclination to do any more than just turn up. Meanwhile, young players were shipped out for bargain basement prices in the seemingly false knowledge that they had to go to save the club from financial strife.

George Graham arrived and quickly worked out that Allardyce and Carr weren't up to the job and whilst he gave the younger players a chance, it was soon evident to him and his assistant Theo Foley that, if the club was to survive, it needed older heads.

In this latest twist, what remained of Millwall's promising young team of the future were now to be overlooked for very different reasons that Anderson had done so.

Under George Petchey the aim was clear: to gradually blood the youngsters with carefully chosen experienced pros that brought something to the team - the likes of Jackson and Kitchener.

Palace had done a similar thing but with the resources to bring in more first team bodies and protect their young stars for longer. Petchey unfortunately didn't have that luxury and paid for it with his job.

Anderson's American model had flopped abysmally as previously explained, and now with the club in such a desperate situation on all fronts, to continue to expose what must have been already psychologically shattered young players to a Third Division relegation scrap was unrealistic and unfair.

Peter Gleasure was the first to be sacrificed. He was sold to Fourth Division Northampton two months into Graham's reign. It was harsh on the young stopper who had always acquitted himself well and was often a victim of constant tinkering with the Millwall back four by Anderson.

Unlike most of that Millwall youth squad, Gleasure was actually scouted from slightly farther afield as part of the opposition during a Luton Schools versus Hackney Schools match.

Gleasure was at Luton Town at the time, during David Pleat's initial tenure, but Bob Pearson was determined to lure him down to The Den and spoke of

Millwall's keenness to sign the stopper with his mum who was a pitchside spectator that day.

That word from Bob was enough to persuade Gleasure to sign schoolboy forms as a 14-year-old. He became an apprentice and took on the regular duties that all apprentices did at the time (except the ones at Palace of course!). He was assigned six pros to look after and boots were kept clean, kit was organised along with training before a 4pm finish and back to his digs in East Dulwich, which was the home of Linda Doyle, partner of Ted Buxton.

Gleasure was a more quiet, but no less impressive figure in Millwall's victorious FA Youth Cup team. His long curly hair became something of a trademark and came about due to a superstition of not getting it cut until they were eliminated from the competition.

He made the successful step up to the first team alongside John Jackson and took over from the legendary stopper to become a first team regular.

His move to Northampton would prove a success where he kept a club record 112 clean sheets in 412 matches, and only two players have made more appearances for the club. He won a Fourth Division championship medal in 1986–87 season and was voted the club's Player of the Season the following season. He enjoyed a career in the game well into the early nineties and now runs a successful driving school.

Gleasure's replacement was the experienced Peter Wells from Southampton, who would soon, somewhat ironically, be ousted by Gleasure's youth team successor Paul Sansome.

The team that eventually escaped the drop into football's basement on the final day of the season by winning at Chesterfield contained just two of the FA Youth Cup winning squad: Paul Robinson and Andy Massey.

That summer Massey and Horrix left for Aldershot and Gillingham respectively and Roberts made the switch across London to Brentford. Graham made no secret of the fact that he favoured experience, shipping promising young striker Teddy Sheringham off to Sweden and early in the 1984/85 season in which Graham guided Millwall to promotion as Division Three runners up, Dave Martin was sold to Wimbledon, leaving Paul Robinson as the sole survivor of the young squad that had promised so much just five years before. Dave Martin's departure was particularly unfortunate, as he had just cemented a place in Graham's first team. Like many of his FA Youth Cup-winning teammates, Martin was in demand during his schoolboy football days.

Already training with West Ham and Coventry, and with other clubs sniffing around as the crucial signing-on date approached, it was inevitable that it would be Bob Pearson that persuaded him to join Millwall.

Martin remembers the tenacity shown by Pearson that left him, like others, in no doubt that Millwall was the place to be:

"Bob came to my house to speak to my mum and dad, it must have been three or four times, and say that Millwall would like to sign me. I knew a few of the boys there anyway as a lot of them played for Poplar Boys which was a Sunday set-up, so when you walked into the place you knew there was fantastic players. We really gelled, it was like a family."

If the beginning of his Millwall career was steady, the end was somewhat more abrupt.

Established in George Graham's starting line-up, Martin, after chatting to a few of the senior pros, decided it was a good time to speak to the manager about improved terms. But as he recalls, George Graham wasn't the easiest man for a young footballer just out of his teens to negotiate with in those pre-agent days:

"I spoke to a couple of the senior players and they said: 'Dave you've got to go in for a pay rise'. So I went to see George, explained that I felt I was doing a good job in the first team and asked if there was any chance of a pay rise."

Of course, Martin, like many of the FA Youth Cup winners, was one of the players signed up to long term contracts, a detail which the wily Graham was quick to point out:

"He said: 'you are doing a good job, but you signed a five year deal didn't you?' so I replied that I knew I was on a five year deal but thought there might be chance now that I was in the first team of a 'thank you'. George just pointed a finger and said: 'the door's over there'."

Despite that, Martin holds no malice toward the Scot.

"Everyone looked up when he walked into a room, he had that swagger about him, but he was a fantastic coach."

Martin was placed on the transfer list after that meeting and before long he was off to Wimbledon.

Ordinary Boys

14

The Bitter End

Paul Robinson's exit was as ignominious as it was probably predictable. Successive managers since Gordon Jago had experienced very different conditions under which to lead the club. Relegation from Division Two amid dire finances, pressure to win promotion out of the Third Division and then even more pressure to escape relegation from it.

None of these situations were conducive to allowing Millwall's carefully constructed youth system to bear the fruit it was intended.

Down the road at Palace, things had gone similarly sour - although at least they'd had the albeit short-lived joy of seeing their young players graduate, win the Second Division title and consolidate themselves in the top flight for at least a season before the vultures swooped on their talented coach Terry Venables and array of young stars - leaving them back in the lower reaches of Division Two. Venables and Fenwick ended up at QPR - ironically where the likes of Jago and Petchey had cut their teeth before moving on to Millwall - and by the mid 1980s, the conveyor belt of footballing talent had seemingly come full circle and returned to Loftus Road.

Probably the most bizarre statistic of all though was the last time most of those young players played together in a Millwall first team.

That Football League Trophy campaign that had started so brightly back in August with those two thumping wins over Brentford and Palace was taken up by the youngsters who Graham had discarded in favour of, understandably, the much more important business of league survival.

A team consisting mainly of the likes of Gleasure, Roberts, Robinson, Massey and later youth recruits Sansome, Stevens, McLeary and Sheringham made it all the way to the final which was played away to promotion-chasing Lincoln.

Just a few weeks after Graham's resurgent first-choice eleven had beaten The Imps 2-1 at The Den, the youngsters brought home another trophy.

It should be pointed out that Graham was by no means against a policy of youth. But in his typically adroit manner, it was all about the immediacy of the job in hand: to ensure Millwall remained a Third Division club, then to re-establish them on a sound footing and get them back that Second Division place that they had lost in 1979. In doing so, he would enhance his reputation as a coach.

Alan Hansen may have had his "you don't win anything with kids" speech rammed down his throat plenty of times, but down in the Third Division in the early eighties, it really needed old heads.

Graham's single-minded approach meant that he made a few mistakes based on first opinions on personalities and snap decisions. One of the more famous ones being releasing Teddy Sheringham. He also allowed Andy Cole to leave during his Arsenal days but he wasn't the first manager to make such a mistake and certainly won't be the last. Unfortunately, he also oversaw the departure of the final member of the class of '79.

Unlike most of his teammates, Paul Robinson's career did not begin at The Den. Spotted district football for Bexley and then North Kent, he was one of seven initially invited by Chelsea to go and train with them.

At the time, like Millwall, the west London club were in dire financial difficulty following the huge investment in the new East Stand at Stamford Bridge, to the point where they lost their Mitcham training ground and up to 40 youngsters could be seen playing on the large forecourt at the front of the stadium. Robinson then received England Youth recognition and had been the subject of interest from West Ham, Spurs, Luton and QPR.

But it was Bob Pearson who managed to persuade Robinson to go to Millwall after seeing him play for Kent in a county match he remembers his first session at Catford mainly for a bizarre meeting with who would be his team captain:

"I turned up for training and Bob Pearson was there with Paul Roberts. He introduced me and said that Paul would be team captain the following season. He left us to go out and train with the rest of the lads and as we set off I noticed Roberts was wearing a pair of moccasin shoes. When I asked if he was actually planning on training in them he just shrugged and said: 'yeah I'll be alright', and he was!".

Although he instantly enjoyed life at Millwall, Robinson's mind was far from made up about who to actually sign schoolboy forms for.

"I was coached by Dario Gradi at Chelsea and he then left to become assistance manager to Colin Murphy at Derby." Robinson recalls.

Derby were a First Division team at the time and Murphy had just taken over from Dave Mackay who had led The Rams to their second league title just two years before. Gradi had obviously remembered Paul from his Chelsea days and was keen to make him one of their first signings as the club looked to rebuild.

Robinson clearly felt he owed Derby first refusal after they had shown faith in him.

"I was travelling up to Derby in school holidays and training with them and I told Bob Pearson that if I didn't sign for Derby then I'd sign for Millwall. Things didn't go well for Murphy at Derby though and he and Gradi were sacked soon after."

In the blink of an eye, Robinson then went from being the target of a First Division side to being courted by one who had just entered the league in the Fourth.

"Dario went to Wimbledon and wanted me to sign for him there, I went one night and thought: 'I'm not playing for this lot', so I signed for Millwall".

If Oscar Arce left an impression on the young players at Millwall, it was an equally impressive coach that made Robinson's decision to join Millwall a little more agonising than his teammates.

"Dario was a great coach, a really, really good coach, but I decided to join Millwall and signed schoolboy forms at the age of 13 in November 1977".

Robinson's memories of the coaching at Millwall were of a much more relaxed environment than at other clubs.

"We weren't really coached as such. I don't think you need someone to get hold of you and say: 'look, this is how you play left-back'. We just trained, I don't think much changed in terms of general training at a football club throughout the fifties and sixties and seventies. In fact, it wasn't until George Graham came that I started to be educated in football."

Before Graham's arrival, Robinson would have a very different footballing education from George Petchey's successor Peter Anderson in a quite bizarre time for the club.

Robinson believes that had the club kept faith with George Petchey he would have turned things around:

"George Petchey just needed time, and the opportunity to bring in a few older heads, but the new Chairman came in, brought in Anderson and started chucking money about".

"Anderson promptly went about dumping the young players, the players he brought in didn't have Millwall at heart and we were all in the reserves."

He remembers that, as with his short tenure at The Den (when it was rumoured he did press conferences naked, fresh from the dressing room) Anderson's departure was particularly bizarre:

"It was a Friday morning and we were training at The Den. I wasn't expecting to be involved, I was just there making up the numbers as you do when you're not in favour. Then just as training finished he came over to me and said: 'come for a run with me'."

"He just darted off around the track around the pitch at the old Den. I caught up with him, expecting him to say something to me but he said nothing. We got back down to the tunnel end and he just turned to me and said: 'do you want to play tomorrow?' I'm thinking: 'what sort of question is that, I'm a footballer, of course I want to play'. I said: 'of course I do' and he ran off down the tunnel and I never saw him again."

The next day Anderson was sacked.

George Graham's arrival at The Den would prove to be the end of Robinson's Millwall days:

"Personally I didn't like the man. He just wasn't very nice. I think because he'd had such a good career himself and we were playing a lower level than he had played at, I think he looked down on us. In fact I used to look forward to the five-a-sides that he played in so I could kick him!"

Robinson was impressed with Graham's coaching however where everyone was given detailed instructions of how they were expected to play and the job they had to do. It would be a system that would, with his trusty right-hand-man Theo Foley, serve him well throughout a successful spell at Arsenal too.

It wasn't all bad under Graham, and Robinson remembers a particularly funny episode after the match that saw Millwall secure their Third Division safety at Chesterfield on the final day of the season:

"We were in the bar afterwards and our chairman Alan Thorne came in. He wasn't a very big bloke and Chesterfield had this big centre half called Bill Green. I think he'd been sent off in the match for head-butting Dean White. Thorne had a beer crate in his hand and walked up to Green, threw the beer crate on the floor in front of him, climbed up on it and thumped him!"

"He was shouting that if he ever did that to one of his players again he'd have him. We had to pull him off him and calm him down!".

Robinson's luck took a turn for the worse when he broke his leg in a pre-season match. It came just when he thought he'd made the breakthrough in Graham's side and he was a regular in the team the previous season. After recovering from the leg break he then suffered an ankle injury.

Several operations later he made his come back but broke down again. He thought he was back to full fitness and flying through his latest comeback match - a reserve game against Fulham at The Den where he was playing in a central midfield role and scored two goals - disaster struck.

"I turned to get a ball in about the 75th minute and just found myself in a heap in the centre circle looking up at the sky and deep down I knew it was over. The club wanted me to retire but I said no. I was determined to get back, but when my contract was up George Graham said: 'you can go'."

Robinson had been at the club for ten years. He was 23 with a mortgage and two children. Rather than persevere with his football career he found a job in the I.T. department at Croydon Council.

Robinson's departure coincided almost immediately with the first return of one of the Class of '79.

With the game slowly collapsing stateside, both Kinsella and Mehmet returned to the UK. Despite their still relatively young years, the opportunity of a big move to the top division seemed to have passed them by being both out of sight and out of mind in what had become something of a footballing circus in the US.

"Me and Dave Mehmet had a week training at Wolves but we weren't over-struck with that" recalls Kinsella.

His gut feeling would prove to be spot on as the Midlands club were at the start of their decline which would see them fall from First to Fourth Division during the next few seasons.

Mehmet opted to accept an offer from Charlton but Kinsella then got that top flight chance to finally join Kevin O'Callaghan when Bobby Robson invited him to train with them. He managed to secure the move and a fee of about £60,000 was agreed with Tampa. Shortly after however, the fates conspired against

Kinsella once again when Robson left to take up the England manager's job.

Kinsella would probably be one of the first to coin a much-heard phrase in the game decades later, but of course about a completely different Fergie:

"Bobby Ferguson came in at Ipswich and I never really saw eye to eye with Fergie".

With his first team opportunities at Ipswich limited, he caught the watchful eye of George Graham and Theo Foley during a reserve match against Chelsea and Kinsella was back at The Den.

Millwall Football club was marking its centenary year but with more problems than parties. Weighed down with fines and all-ticket restrictions from the Football Association following trouble during a home match against Leeds and a crippling £1 million bill to bring the crumbling old Den up to safety standards, it was in a worse state than at any time in its eventful history and nobody felt like celebrating.

George Graham left to take his dream job at Highbury, star striker John Fashanu was sold to Wimbledon on transfer deadline day - against Graham's wishes - and would be part of a Dons team that would go on to win promotion to the top flight at the end of that season along with Millwall's local rivals Charlton.

That really stung. Wimbledon had been elected to the Football League in 1977 - at the same time that Millwall's talented young side was being coached by

Oscar Arce and should have been the foundation to see Millwall in the top flight for the first time in their history.

Wimbledon had managed to achieve in less than ten years what Millwall still hadn't managed in 100. Now it felt they were further away than ever.

Tony Kinsella's brief reunion was ended that summer by a move to non-league Enfield, unlike many of his fellow FA Youth Cup winners, he would go on to stay in the game, earn his coaching badges and is still coaching today.

The on-going financial crisis at the club saw a clamber for players toward the exit doors, these were desperate times, and there only seemed to be one way again - as in 1979: down, but with seemingly no prospect of young players making the breakthrough to help the club this time. John Docherty was brought in as manager, a move that angered most fans as it appeared to be a cost-cutting exercise, which of course it was.

There was a new chairman at the helm: Reg Burr. Unlike Thorne, he made no elaborate promises, but told it as it was. The club was on its uppers once again.

The class of '79 had finally all gone. Then, as Docherty assessed what the club had and what he had to do, something strange happened:

They started to come back.

Ordinary Boys

15

When Life Gives You Lemons…

John Docherty arrived at Millwall under no illusions. He had built a reputation for taking Cambridge United on little or no resources from the Fourth Division to the Second, but expectation and patience at Millwall would be about as far away from that at The Abbey Stadium as you could get.

Following a rather uneventful spell as number two to Frank McLintock at Brentford, he arrived at Millwall to find the cupboard bare.

Showing Teddy Sheringham the door was one of George Graham's last moves as Millwall manager, and Docherty promptly invited him right back in.

If Graham didn't feel the youth at the club could cut it, Docherty didn't agree, but then he wasn't exactly in a position to make a choice.

Docherty knew that, unlike Anderson, he had to quickly grasp what made Millwall tick - on and off the pitch. He clearly relished the challenge and was not put off by the frightening response he received from a bleak early home defeat to Bradford.

September 1986 was probably an all time low for Millwall. In driving rain, The Den looking a sorry sight with half of it being closed due to the ongoing essential ground improvements demanded by the GLC, just over 3,000 fans witnessed a woeful surrender to a very average Bradford side. It was a third successive defeat but proved something of a watershed.

So far that season Docherty had used two goalkeepers - both products of Millwall's youth system. One was the now almost veteran Paul Sansome and the other Brian Horne. Of the other twelve players deployed by Docherty, seven were home grown players: Keith Stevens, Nicky Coleman, Alan McLeary, Teddy Sheringham, Michael Marks, Darren Morgan and Dave Mehmet.

Mehmet had rejoined The Lions that summer. His American adventure over, he returned the UK for a brief spell at Charlton before moving to Gillingham where he scored 32 goals in just over 100 appearances for the Kent club and when Docherty made the approach he didn't need asking twice.

He was soon followed by Phil Coleman, whose younger brother Nicky was by now a regular at left back. Phil had enjoyed a spell in Finland with

MYPA45 where he'd collected a league champions medal.

By the end of the season, John Docherty had managed to succeed where George Petchey had fallen short almost a decade before. He had managed to build a side that contained a careful balance of youth and experience.

Strikers Sheringham and Marks led the goalscoring charts with 16 and 10 goals respectively with both managing to score their first hat-tricks for the club before Christmas. The low of that Bradford defeat was never revisited as fans started to latch on to Docherty's philosophy.

Experience was brought in to offer a protective foil and education for the youngsters in the shape of Gerry Armstrong and Paul Hinshelwood but the real coup for Docherty was to secure the services of a certain Terry Hurlock from Reading who, alongside Les Briley in the midfield, also helped to ensure Millwall's new young Lions were never left as exposed as their predecessors.

Danis Salman also provided useful experience and the youth angle was further bolstered by the capture of winger Jimmy Carter who had been released by QPR.

Docherty's Lions never dipped into the bottom half of the Second Division table after their 1-1 draw at Birmingham in the last game of 1986 until an end-of-season slump that saw them finish 16th. In fact, for a brief spell, they even flirted with the notion of making an appearance in the first ever play-off competition.

Victory over Sheffield United at The Den in February saw them jump to seventh, just two places from the fifth spot that would have seen them face the third-bottom side in Division One in the early format of the competition. But it was a bridge too far for such a small and inexperienced squad and three subsequent defeats put an end to that.

Mehmet's Millwall return, as with Phil Coleman's, would prove to be a short cameo blighted by injuries. They were coming to the end of their careers but their presence in that new, up-and-coming team that Docherty was building would have almost certainly proved an invaluable link between youth and experience - and the Millwall way.

Mehmet would return to the club again in a coaching capacity along with Kevin O'Callaghan. Working with the club's youth academy, they would oversee another pride of young Lions that included the likes of Cahill, Reid, and Ifill.

Mehmet, who was at the academy for twelve years, believes Millwall have made fatal errors with their youth policy today having relinquished their elite academy status in an attempt to save the £1 million annual cost in favour of more traditional first team building.

The money was instead used by then manager Kenny Jackett on wages for loans of experienced players. An exercise which worked in the short-term, preserving Millwall's second tier status for a few seasons, but long term has, in Mehmet's opinion, damaged the future of the club and its chances of bringing through new home-grown talent.

"It took ten years to get top academy status, Bob Pearson fought to get that status, it took ten years to get it, but just one day to lose it again. The top young players around here are going to Charlton and Palace instead these days"

Back in 1987 however, things were finally falling into place. For Millwall's long-suffering fans there was more than a hint of trepidation though.

In many respects, they were potentially making the same mistakes that had been made when Peter Anderson had been given so much freedom to bring in his own players - most of whom proved to be not only well past their best, unaware of why they were there, and happy to merely go through the motions.

Docherty however was using an entirely different approach. Rather than just signing them up, his recruits were often subject to quite unorthodox methods of persuasion.

In fact, legend has it that when Tony Cascarino was sat opposite The Doc in his Den office discussing the finer points of the Gillingham striker's Millwall deal, both Leeds and Ipswich made last-ditch attempts to gazump The Lions his signature. Docherty's response was to hand the telephone to Cascarino and allow him to hear what they had to offer. By the end of the day Cascarino was a Millwall player.

The critical factor by which any Millwall manager has succeeded or failed is to understand the culture of the club and its fans. It may sound obvious, but in the modern era, where football clubs are businesses and managers brought in on the understanding that an often unrealistic level of success is achieved, many are able to walk into a club with their entourage and dictate how they want literally every aspect of the organisation to run.

Those that meet with resistance usually find it at boardroom level where an ego-maniac owner insists on interfering. Sometimes it is met at fan level. Any manager trying to impose himself on the club at Millwall has always felt the full force of the latter.

Ian Holloway's explanation for his failure at Millwall was that the club "didn't get him", and in those three simple words was his downfall. He, like Anderson, pretended to "get" Millwall, but it didn't work, the fans aren't that easily duped. George Graham found the perfect balance at a time when the club seemed destined for oblivion, Kenny Jackett's reign was similar.

Neil Harris learned, like Keith Stevens and Alan McLeary, that club legend status will only last so long too.

Speaking in 1988, manager John Docherty said of the club:

"Millwall are one of the few clubs who have retained the style that reflects their area, their people. The difference is the locality, and the feeling that the community does relate to the football club. It probably goes back to when the team was associated with dockers.

"Generations later, we still get their descendants coming to watch the team from places as far afield as St Neots, and Southampton. The club means so much to them. I am very conscious of that. Especially last year, when we won promotion. I was very conscious of what that meant to people who had stood on the terraces here for 40 years.

"Being deprived of success, I think Millwall fans went through a period of having an isolationist view, a siege mentality. It is only in the last two years that we have started to bring them out of that, and give

them something to be proud of. That coincided with success on the field.

"We got that by working with the characteristics of the club, particularly those that related to the area. If you have a competitive team at this club, you reflect the area. If there is a sincerity about the Millwall team you build, if it is honest, you are identifying with this area. If it is a team which is proud to wear the shirt, you are identifying with this area.

"My job is to give this area a team it can feel pride in, and one that can also be successful. "But you've got to be sensible about this. From the media point of view this is a deprived, hard area that is looked on as being difficult. So they think that a hard and dour team that is produced from such an area must be symbolic of it.

"They categorise Millwall in that way. But if you look deeper into the community, you see the warmth, you see the friendliness, and the sincerity of the people. You have to get those elements into the side as well. It is a mixture.

"In practical terms this means Millwall fans like the big, archetypal centre-half, good and dominating in the air, and they like the classic centre-forward, big and bustling, getting into the penalty area. But they

also admire subtlety and skill on the ball. They have always had ball-playing wingers here.

"Traditionally, they have always had teams which tend to be a blend, people who will give them a hundred per cent, but at the same time, there will be players with skill in the team. If you get that blend right, you can achieve more than you might think possible.

"The things that appeal to this crowd, as I see it, also appeal to me. In many ways, I have joined a club which suits my personality and ideals. When I look at a potential player, I think 'Is he a Millwall player?' A player has to fit, not necessarily into the locality, but into the identity of the club.

"I have always wanted to know the history of any club I played for. At Brentford, I was fortunate enough to find a couple of scrapbooks, with details of former players, and so forth. Wherever I have been, I swot up the history of the area. This creates a bond, it helps you reach an affinity with the city or town, and the club itself. Sheffield United had a lot of Yorkshire-born players. They had a great fervour for playing for the local team. This sustains you. In adversity, you come closer together.

"No matter how successful we become, we have got to build on our close liaison with the community. In the early days, there is no great difficulty in going out into the community. But when you become successful, going out into the community can pose problems.

Everybody wants to know you then. Whereas before it was you who was going to them, and encouraging them. We have to make sure that community work does not infringe on what we do professionally. But providing we understand that, I think the two work naturally together.

"What players do in the community keeps their feet on the ground, it prevents us getting too far away from our roots. This club is taking football back to its roots, and we all benefit from that."

It's a piece that couldn't have been better worded had it been written by a fan himself. It could also have been jointly penned by the hands of Gordon Jago and George Petchey. It spoke of their own beliefs in producing a Millwall team that had the culture and DNA of the club indelibly ingrained in it, where its players played with the same heart and determination that the fans on the terraces cheered them on with. The same fight and camaraderie of the Class of '79.

In John Docherty, Millwall had, it seemed, found an ideal, if highly unlikely candidate to finish the work started by Jago and Petchey.

And finish it he most certainly did.

Ordinary Boys

Ordinary Boys

Extra Time

Ordinary Boys

Full Circle

The Class of 1979 *should* have been the foundation for Millwall's first ever First Division team, but events conspired against them and many fans felt their team were fated to remain the only London club never to have graced Division One.

In 1987, with the club once again in dire financial trouble, a welcome wind of change swept through The Den. A shirt sponsorship deal with Lewisham Council and a new board who made available an unprecedented transfer war chest to manager John Docherty saw new faces arrive - and some familiar ones too.

Already there was Coleman and Mehmet. They were joined by striker Tony Cascarino, defender Steve Wood, winger George Lawrence and a certain Kevin O'Callaghan.

O'Callaghan arrived via Ipswich and Portsmouth - with a stop-off at Hollywood in between. He enjoyed five successful years at Portman Road, making 115 appearances and gaining international recognition with The Republic of Ireland. Within a year of signing for Robson's Tractor Boys, he was starring alongside Sylvester Stallone, Michael Caine and Pele in cult football film *Escape to Victory*. He joined Portsmouth in 1985 and helped them to promotion to the First Division in 1987 before the call came from Millwall.

The 1987-88 season saw Millwall field one of the most home-grown first-team line-ups in the club's history. Brian Horne in goal and defenders Nicky Coleman, Keith Stevens and Alan McLeary were all products of The Lions' rejuvenated youth system. With O'Callaghan in midfield and Teddy Sheringham up front, over half of Millwall's starting eleven had made the step up through the ranks. With Phil Coleman and Mehmet still in the squad and the likes of Darren Morgan and Sean Sparham ready to graduate too, the dream that had been born a decade before under the watchful eye of Gordon Jago, Oscar Arce, George Petchey and David Payne seemed to finally be coming true.

On May 2nd 1988 at Boothferry Park, home of Hull City, Millwall were awarded a penalty in the eleventh minute of the match - their penultimate of the season. Kevin O'Callaghan converted the spot-kick and the match ended 1-0 to Millwall. It was a win that sealed not just promotion to Division One for the first time in the club's 103 year history, but the Second Division Championship too.

It had been a much longer, and far more eventful journey than anyone could have imagined during that idyllic summer of 1977 when an eccentric, football-mad Argentinian taught a group of captivated youngsters how to do keepie-ups with a tennis ball as they devoured ham and cheese rolls.

It may have a been a mainly different team to that one that lifted the FA Youth Cup, but the same spirit was there, the same camaraderie and love for the game, and for Millwall Football Club.

In many ways, the class of '79 had finally come of age.

Ordinary Boys

Dean Horrix

Five of Millwall's FA Youth Cup winning side left the club only to return. The last of those was Dean Horrix. Horrix was a classy front man who had been spotted at the age of nine playing for Slough Rockets by Bob Pearson – close to his own home turf.

Pearson made sure that his signature was secured and he was a goalscoring regular in the Millwall side during the FA Youth Cup winning season until that horrendous injury at Forest in the quarter final.

Horrix made a successful transition to the Millwall first team and continued to score goals but was one of the players that left after George Graham arrived.

Many fans felt letting him go was a big mistake and this seemed to be proved when, after a brief spell at Gillingham he joined Reading and enjoyed five successful years there scoring 35 goals in 158 appearances as the team won promotion to the Second Division. Midway through Millwall's first ever First

Division season he returned to The Den as understudy to the prolific striking partnership of Tony Cascarino and Teddy Sheringham.

Their form and good luck with injuries meant Horrix's first team opportunities were limited, although a four match suspension for Sheringham towards the end of the season saw him start four matches against Manchester United, Liverpool, West Ham and Tottenham, making him the second of the Class of '79 to play for the club in the top flight.

In the match against Liverpool at The Den he almost crowned his comeback with a goal but saw a spectacular volley rattle Bruce Grobbelaar's bar.

Later on in the following season Horrix moved to Bristol City who were looking to seal promotion from Division Three.

On March 11th 1990, just hours after helping his new club cement their place at the top of the division with a 1-0 win at Shrewsbury, Horrix died when the car he was travelling in, driven by his wife Carol, crashed into trees on a main road close to their Basingstoke home. Carol was seriously injured.

A promptly-arranged Friends of Millwall Dinner raised over £11,000 for the fund set up to help support Horrix's widow and two young children.

An end-of-season testimonial was staged at The Den where Paul Gascoigne agreed to play – just weeks before setting off to play for Bobby Robson's

England in the 1990 World Cup finals in Italy. In fact, it is believed that Gascoigne was the first to agree to appear in the match and didn't need a moment's hesitation to say 'yes'.

It was a mark of the respect everyone in the game had for Dean Horrix.

Ordinary Boys

George Petchey

George Petchey was born in Whitechapel, London. He joined West Ham in 1948 at the age of 17 and, as a wing-half, made three appearances for the club before being transferred to QPR in 1953.

He made his Rangers debut against Brighton in August 1953 and over the next seven seasons, played 255 league games for Rangers scoring 22 goals.

Petchey earned a reputation as a tough-tackling, hard-working defensive midfielder who could also pass the ball with vision and accuracy.

In 1960 Petchey moved to Crystal Palace. He made 143 appearances for Palace scoring 12 goals. He was ever present as Palace achieved promotion in 1961 but suffered a serious eye injury which would shorten his playing career. He returned from the injury in a home FA Cup quarter final against Leeds in 1965, and made one further appearance in the league, the following month. He retired to become coach at Crystal Palace and then manager at Leyton Orient.

He was appointed Millwall manager in 1978 and guided the club to Second Division safety. He was unable to prevent relegation the following season but as the 1979-80 season began, Petchey was finally able to make his own mark on the Millwall squad, bringing in experienced players to compliment the members of the FA Youth Cup winning squad that were now regulars in the first team.

Millwall spent most of the first few months of the season in the Third Division promotion places but the forced sale of Kevin O'Callaghan at the start of 1980 made his task almost impossible.

Petchey was replaced by Peter Anderson at the end of 1980.

It is widely believed that, although Petchey's time at The Den coincided with some of the club's leanest years, had the club kept faith with him and supported him in the transfer market he would have been the man to continue developing the club's young players and see their transition through to the first team and ultimate success on the pitch. After leaving Millwall, Petchey joined Brighton as coach and also had a spell as first team manager. George Petchey was the first

English coach to obtain all of the available UEFA coaching badges.

During his earlier spell at Orient he was responsible for bringing Laurie Cunningham through the ranks and went on to the role of Chief Scout at Newcastle United in the late 1990s under Ruud Gullit and then one of the first team coaches at St James Park under Sir Bobby Robson.

Ordinary Boys

Dean Horrix
21 November 1961 – 11 March 1990

George Petchey
24 June 1931 - 23 December 2019

Ordinary Boys

A Different Game

On February 27th, 2020, Millwall's youth team travelled to Stamford Bridge to play Chelsea in the quarter finals of the FA Youth Cup.

Their 1-0 defeat saw them come agonisingly close to achieving one of the club's best showings in the competition against opposition with resources way beyond their own. Resources that have helped Chelsea dominate the competition, winning seven of the last ten finals - almost all by large victories.

For Millwall's 2020 youth team squad, it was every bit as impressive an achievement as the final win in 1979 - such is the size of the gulf between the top teams and the rest of the league now. Since the inception of the Premier League almost 30 years ago, just one team from outside the top flight has won the FA Youth Cup - Ipswich in 2005. Millwall became the first team from outside the top flight to reach the final in the Premier League era, losing to Arsenal in the 1994 final.

They had won the competition for a second time in 1991 when they beat Sheffield Wednesday 3-0 in the only final to feature two teams from outside the top flight. Unfortunately, as in 1979, the financial state of the club dictated once more that most of the players from that team would be sold before the club could reap the benefits from them.

The second team from outside the top flight to reach the final since the formation of the Premier League was Crystal Palace in 1997. Apart from that, only one other team from outside the Premier League (Sheffield United) have reached the final. With the Football League represented by just three teams in the last 27 years of finals (eight featured in the 17 finals before that) the Premier League continues to dominate not just the senior game but football at youth level too - which is the life blood for most of the teams outside the top flight.

Millwall Football Club, like the game itself, has changed dramatically since the 1970s. The structure of the club is geared towards development of its own home-grown talent, yet you could only really point to two occasions in its history when it has truly benefitted at first team level. In many ways, the 1988 Second Division championship-winning season owed a lot to

Millwall's youth policy as described elsewhere in this book.

In 2001 Millwall won the third tier title with a team that many argue is the best Lions side to have been assembled in the modern era.

Thanks to the club's academy - which employed Kevin O'Callaghan and Dave Mehmet amongst its team of coaches - a side containing the likes of Steven Reid, Paul Ifill, Tim Cahill, Richard Sadlier, Joe Dolan and Marc Bircham who were all products of the academy took the club up in 2001 and to within a match of the Premier League in 2002.

In the game today it is harder than ever to attract local young footballers to Millwall as many are snared by the big clubs at an early age from the very doorstep that Bob Pearson used to patrol so efficiently. Even once signed, the best prospects are often the subject of multi-million pound transfers by the top Premier League clubs at the age of just 16 before they have even come close to appearing in the first team. Most of those players never actually make a first team appearance in the top flight and end up reappearing a few years later in League Two, non-league or, disillusioned, they leave the game altogether. Class of '79 striker Chris Dibble believes that, had the facilities, resources and expertise available to clubs today been around in 1979, that team would have been able to truly realise its potential - whether it was at Millwall or elsewhere. It's hard to argue with that. Millwall are one of just seven different teams from outside the top flight to win the FA Youth Cup and the only one to have won it on two separate occasions (1979 and 1991 as opposed to Crystal Palace's back-to-back wins in 1977 and 1978). It's unlikely that any team outside the Premier League will ever match that.

Today, scouting is very different too. The Bob Pearsons and Arnie Warrens of the world have been replaced by young technicians with tablets, laptops and software algorithms to search out footballing talent.

Young footballers are put through endless regular tests to ascertain physical development and those not thought to be progressing in the desired manner - or according to the charts' and spreadsheets' recommended levels are turned away.

Football clubs no longer have to wait until their chosen young stars of the future have finished their studies before signing them up.

Instead they are given special leave of their regular studies with their classmates and spend long periods of time taking lessons within the confines of their club.

For these young men there are no Saturday morning matches for their school, or Sunday junior league enjoyment of the game. There is little or no gradual progression with their peers through to schools area finals, county level competition or district recognition.

For the young footballers of today, playing the game they love - if they are good enough to suggest they can do so for a living - means around the clock dedication to every minute detail from the age of as young as six until for many, they decide they don't actually love the game after all.

Professional football it seems is no longer a game for ordinary boys.

That love never died for the likes of Peter Gleasure, Dave Martin, Paul Roberts, Phil Coleman, Paul Robinson, Tony Kinsella, Ian Gale, Dave Mehmet, Alan McKenna, Chris Dibble, Kevin O'Callaghan, Dean Horrix, Andy Massey, Tony Dark, Dave Hockley or John Helps.

Alan McKenna remained in the game. He enjoyed spells at Berwick and Arbroath, played in Australia, qualified as a Class Two referee and after officiating for several years, took up Bob Pearson on his offer to scout for Millwall.

He then made a string of useful scouting contacts and went on to work in that capacity for Nottingham Forest and Barnsley.

He walked away from his final scouting job at Hearts when he rejected the modern approach to that aspect of the game. The statistics, spreadsheets and overanalysis to him, quite rightly, wasn't football and I think he sums it up perfectly:

"Everything's a stat now, but you know what? I've never seen anybody make a footballer out of a stat. All the skill in the world won't make a difference without hard work and love for the game. As long as you have the heart and the love for the game to go with that skill, and you work for 90 minutes for the shirt, you'll do OK"

Ordinary Boys

The FA Youth Cup

Year	Winners	Score	Runners–up
1952–53	Manchester United	9–3	Wolves
1953–54	Manchester United	5–4	Wolves
1954–55	Manchester United	7–1	WBA
1955–56	Manchester United	4–3	Chesterfield
1956–57	Manchester United	8–2	West Ham United
1957–58	Wolves	7–6	Chelsea
1958–59	Blackburn Rovers	2–1	West Ham United
1959–60	Chelsea	5–2	Preston North End
1960–61	Chelsea	5–3	Everton
1961–62	Newcastle United	2–1	Wolves
1962–63	West Ham United	6–5	Liverpool
1963–64	Manchester United	5–2	Swindon Town
1964–65	Everton	3–2	Arsenal
1965–66	Arsenal	5–3	Sunderland
1966–67	Sunderland	2–0	Birmingham City
1967–68	Burnley	3–2	Coventry City
1968–69	Sunderland	6–3	WBA
1969–70	Tottenham	1–1	Coventry City replay 2–2, 2nd replay 1–0
1970–71	Arsenal	2–0	Cardiff City
1971–72	Aston Villa	5–2	Liverpool
1972–73	Ipswich Town	4–1	Bristol City
1973–74	Tottenham	2–1	Huddersfield Town
1974–75	Ipswich Town	5–1	West Ham United
1975–76	WBA	5–0	Wolves
1976–77	Crystal Palace	1–0	Everton
1977–78	Crystal Palace	1–0	Aston Villa
1978–79	Millwall	2–0	Manchester City
1979–80	Aston Villa	3–2	Manchester City
1980–81	West Ham United	2–1	Tottenham
1981–82	Watford	7–6	Manchester United
1982–83	Norwich City	6–5	Everton Aggregated extra time
1983–84	Everton	4–2	Stoke City

Ordinary Boys

1984–85	Newcastle United	4–1	Watford
1985–86	Manchester City	3–1	Manchester United
1986–87	Coventry City	2–1	Charlton Athletic
1987–88	Arsenal	6–1	Doncaster Rovers
1988–89	Watford	2–1	Manchester City Aggregated extra time
1989–90	Tottenham	3–2	Middlesbrough
1990–91	Millwall	3–0	Sheffield Wednesday
1991–92	Manchester United	6–3	Crystal Palace
1992–93	Leeds United	4–1	Manchester United
1993–94	Arsenal	5–3	Millwall
1994–95	Manchester United	1–1	Tottenham 4–2 pens
1995–96	Liverpool	4–1	West Ham United
1996–97	Leeds United	3–1	Crystal Palace
1997–98	Everton	5–3	Blackburn Rovers
1998–99	West Ham United	9–0	Coventry City
1999–00	Arsenal	5–1	Coventry City
2000–01	Arsenal	6–3	Blackburn Rovers
2001–02	Aston Villa	4–2	Everton
2002–03	Manchester United	3–1	Middlesbrough
2003–04	Middlesbrough	4–0	Aston Villa
2004–05	Ipswich Town	3–2	Southampton Aggregated extra time
2005–06	Liverpool	3–2	Manchester City
2006–07	Liverpool	2–2	Manchester United 4–3 pens
2007–08	Manchester City	4–2	Chelsea
2008–09	Arsenal	6–2	Liverpool
2009–10	Chelsea	3–2	Aston Villa
2010–11	Manchester United	6–3	Sheffield United
2011–12	Chelsea	4–1	Blackburn Rovers
2012–13	Norwich City	4–2	Chelsea
2013–14	Chelsea	7–6	Fulham
2014–15	Chelsea	5–2	Manchester City
2015–16	Chelsea	4–2	Manchester City
2016–17	Chelsea	6–2	Manchester City
2017–18	Chelsea	7–1	Arsenal
2018–19	Liverpool	1–1	Manchester City 5–3 pens

Also by the author:

August 1988. The second Summer of Love. The UK wasn't basking in a heatwave, but the euphoric mix of acid house, rave and psychedelia meant that most were completely oblivious to the weather anyway. A year that had started like any other had blossomed in a feel good factor not experienced since the sixties. Love was in the air, house prices were up, unemployment was down and Millwall were in the First Division...

The Lions' appearance at football's top table for the first time in their 103 year history is probably best compared with Punk than Rave culture. Exploding on the scene and sticking two fingers up to the establishment, shocking their way to the top of the pile before being chewed up and spat out and then disappearing as quickly as they had arrived. But this was 1988 not 1976 and while their somewhat unwelcome arrival was no less dramatic and explosive than the opening chords to Anarchy in The UK, there was little bit more class about these boys as they slotted into the high life to the assured but no less revolutionary backing track of Voodoo Ray.

This is the story of a humble south London football club and its unique fans. How a team, built on a shoestring budget and made up largely of locals and boyhood Millwall supporters stunned the football world for a brief but beautiful time back in 1988 when football really was the beautiful game. For two years Millwall rubbed shoulders with the game's elite. Their fans, when they weren't raving in fields or warehouses, were gleefully gatecrashing a party where only the wealthy usually received an invite. There was delight and disappointment, triumph and tragedy, but what a ride.

During the late eighties, the drug of choice was Ecstasy, but for many, just following Millwall was enough, a truly natural high. With contributions from members of that historic Millwall squad as well as fans and opposition players and fans, this is a footballing tale that will never be repeated. Enjoy this trip, and it is a trip...

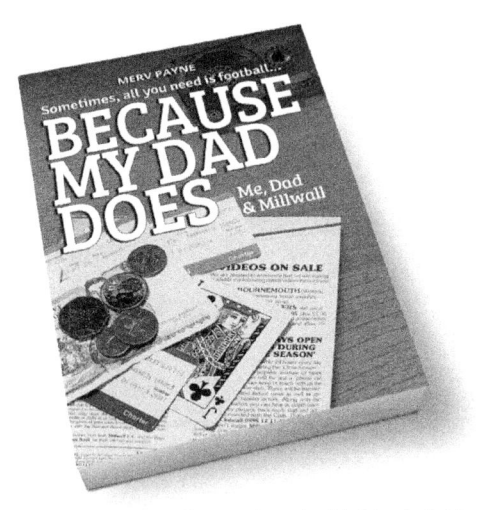

Merv was determined to forge a bond with his dad. It's usually the other way around, but he could tell from a very young age that he'd probably have to do most of the work himself.

After going to their first football match together when he was seven, a shared passion began that would last the rest of their lives - which is just as well, because they had very little else to cement their bond.

Merv's attempts to enhance this relationship through junior football almost had disastrous consequences, but their passion for football – and in particular Millwall – became the glue that held them together.

What Merv really wanted was to share unique, unprecedented success at Millwall with his dad – something that was very thin on the ground in the early eighties. What they both wanted more than anything was to see their team in the First Division for the first time.

Because My Dad Does is a nostalgic journey through the days of the terraces, following your team - with and without your dad - on teletext or the football special, and sharing a once-in-a-lifetime, never-to-be-repeated football season as father and son.

Both titles available now in paperback or Kindle

format at

amazon

Or buy online at:

www.anaturalhighmillwall.co.uk